THE
HARPER'S INDEX
BOOK

D0048566

THE HARPER'S INDEX BOOK

◆

Lewis H. Lapham
Michael Pollan
Eric Etheridge

◆

Illustrated by Martim Avillez
With an introduction by Lewis H. Lapham
Research directed by Pamela Abrams

An Owl Book

HENRY HOLT AND COMPANY
NEW YORK

Published by Henry Holt and Company, Inc.,
521 Fifth Avenue, New York, New York 10175.
Distributed in Canada by Fitzhenry & Whiteside Limited,
195 Allstate Parkway, Markham, Ontario L3R 4T8.

Library of Congress Cataloging in Publication Data
Lapham, Lewis H.
The Harper's index book.
"An Owl book."
1. Handbooks, vade-mecums, etc. 2. Statistics.
I. Pollan, Michael. II. Etheridge, Eric. III. Title.
AG105.L33   1986   031'.02   86–33549
ISBN 0-8050-0325-8 (pbk.)

Designer: Ann Gold
Printed in the United States of America

CONTENTS

ACKNOWLEDGMENTS

Virtually everyone connected with *Harper's Magazine* over the last three years has had a hand in the making of this book, but several people deserve to be singled out. Charis Conn helped direct a herculean research effort. The research staff included Billie Fitzpatrick, Cathryn Harding, J. Gregory Jones, Valerie Leleu, Alane Mason, Henry Sidel, Ilena Silverman, Louise Sloan, and Fareed Zakaria.

The monthly "Harper's Index," from which the book has been adapted, is a collaborative enterprise and wouldn't be possible without the regular participation of the following members of the staff: Janet Gold, Richard Marin, Gerald Marzorati, Ann Stern, Terry Teachout, Randall Warner, and Martin Morse Wooster.

Thanks also to David Corn, Mark Edmundson, Elena Gustines, Rick MacArthur, Deborah Rust, Shelia Wolfe, Kate Browne, Judith Belzer, Doug Ellis, Elvira Lopez, Victoria Reisenbach, Mary Anne Malley, Karen Rydzewski, Kathryn Crowley, Max Lane, Benjamin Glassberg, Joseph Malits, Lynne Bertrand, Anne Hardart, Lisa Levchuk, and all those interns, friends, and readers who have suggested statistics over the years.

LHL, MP, EE

INTRODUCTION

Numbers can be made to tell as many stories as a crooked
lawyer or an old comedian. They can prove a theory or
wreck a government, arrange a marriage or steal a fortune.
Among all the world's peoples, none take as much delight
in numbers as do the Americans, who, if given the option,
would rather believe a number than a fairy tale. To an
American, a statistic or a percentage point counts as a
closing argument, a proof of virtue or the judgment of
heaven.

Harper's Index sets numbers to the task of taking
soundings. Every month, *Harper's Magazine* publishes the
Index as a single page of numbers that measure, one way or
another, the drifting tide of events. The list might note the
number of people in Florida on the waiting list to see an
execution (215), the price of a 1909 Honus Wagner
baseball card ($32,000), the average weight of male bears
in Alaska (250 pounds) and Pennsylvania (487 pounds), or
the number of New York City police officers who belong to
the Screen Actors Guild (350).

Taken separately or together, or sometimes in
juxtaposition (i.e., "Amount the Reagan administration
budgeted for military bands in 1987: $154,200,000/
Amount it budgeted for the National Endowment for the
Arts: $144,900,000"), the month's representative numbers
form a kind of plumb line cast into the infinite sea of
numbers. In no way definitive, the Index offers fragmentary

proofs of the world's density, wonder, contradiction, and desire.

As published in *Harper's Magazine* since March 1984, the Index has attracted a large and friendly crowd of readers who accept its premises and laugh at its jokes. It was perhaps the most radical of the new journalistic forms introduced three years ago as part of the magazine's new design, and it is now reprinted, in whole or in part, by 18 American newspapers as well as by newspapers and magazines in Germany, Italy, Spain, France, Portugal, Greece, and Japan. A fair number of publications have borrowed the device without bothering to send money or assign credit, and some of the less controversial numbers—"Life span of a baseball in a major-league game (in pitches): 5"—have made guest appearances, again without attribution, on network television.

The magazine's editors employ two systems of acquiring numbers for the Index. First and most obviously, they sift through the reams of published data (government reports, trade journals, weekly magazines, opinion polls, corporate statements, foundation studies, etc.) that accumulate every month in the magazine's offices like the wood shavings on the floor of a lumber mill. The editors also encounter stray numbers in cocktail-party conversations, or in their random reading of a novel, an airline ticket, or a menu. The magazine's readers send additional numbers. Having learned to admire the Index, they contribute unsolicited statistics as miscellaneous as their own lines of interest or logic.

All these first-degree numbers belong to the category of "found objects"—bits and pieces of things that might or might not fit the specifications of some larger design. Once submitted to the magazine's methods of verification, a good many numbers prove to be wrong, but the process of tracing them to their points of origin not infrequently leads to the discovery of other numbers even more curious and strange.

If roughly half the numbers published in any one month's Index derive from given data, the remainder follow from questions asked by editors trying to find a moral in a numeral. What, an editor once asked, might the Index add to (or subtract from) the sum of news and gossip then attendant upon "Miami Vice"? Why not compare the budget of the television show against the budget of the actual Miami Police vice squad? A series of telephone calls—to NBC, to the Miami Police Department, to *Variety*, and to a number of other informants—resulted in this juxtaposition: "Budget per episode of 'Miami Vice': $1,500,000. Annual budget of the Miami vice squad $1,161,741."

e. e. cummings once defined poetry as the art of "asking the more beautiful question," and as often as not the Index numbers serve as metaphors, acquiring literary value by reason of the questions they ask or the images they retrieve from the abyss. Perceived as a collection of notes and sketches or, more fancifully, as an anthology of very brief tales, the Index accommodates itself to as many interpretations as can be constructed by the English Department at Yale.

The casting of the Harper's Index as a book offered an entirely new set of possible themes and variations. Organized in the form of a philosophical dictionary, the numbers combine into minor essays. The more abstract the word under definition (*Appearances, Hegemony, Realpolitik,* etc.) the more easily it accommodates metaphor. Thus, statistics about subjects as diverse as Coca-Cola, sex, and the military budget all find a place under the rubric "Appetites." The device allows the Index to preserve its tone and character as well as its capacity for not-so-random commentary.

The compiling of the dictionary delighted its editors with a sense of further discovery. With any luck, the readers also will take pleasure in still another kind of story that numbers, properly instructed, can be made to tell.

LHL

THE
HARPER'S INDEX
BOOK

ADDITIONS

Silicone breast implant operations performed in the United States in 1986: 115,000

Percentage increase in the number of U.S. millionaires since 1980: 145

Percentage increase in the number of gangs in Los Angeles in 1986: 20

Average weekly increase in the population of state and federal prisons in 1986: 1,000

Cost of building a new maximum security prison, per cell: $75,600

Number of backyard swimming pools in 1977: 1,330,000

Today: 2,130,000

Percentage increase in the heat of the sun in the last 3.5 million years: 25

Pounds of hazardous waste generated per capita in the United States in 1950: 4.6

Today: 2,600

Hospices in the United States in 1980: 269

Today: 1,500

Number of Catholic churches under construction in Poland: 1,000

Percentage increase in the membership of the Mormon Church since 1976: 60

Number of manufacturing jobs New England has gained since 1982: 54,450

New books acquired yearly by Yale University libraries (in miles of shelf space): 4

Consumer marketing studies published every day in the United States: 8

Total memory capacity produced by the U.S. computer industry in 1986 (in kilobytes): 449,600,000,000

ALARMS

Deaths caused by terrorism, worldwide, in 1979: 1,963

In 1985: 7,166

False warnings of a nuclear attack on the United States in the past eight years: 6

Estimated number of countries that possess chemical weapons: 16

Pounds of plutonium and highly enriched uranium that are missing from U.S. inventories: 9,600

Pounds of plutonium needed to make an atomic bomb: 15

Shipments of hazardous materials made in the United States each day: 500,000

Portion of all vehicles carrying hazardous materials that are incorrectly labeled: 1/4

Percentage of Japanese with IQs above 130: 10

Percentage of Americans: 2

Percentage of U.S. women between 20 and 24 in 1965 who were infertile: 4

Percentage of women between 20 and 24 who are infertile today: 11

Percentage increase in cases of tuberculosis reported in New York City in 1985: 14

Percentage of New York City children who live below the poverty line: 40

Months it will take for the number of AIDS cases to double: 12

Number of U.S. banks classified as "problems" by the FDIC: 1,439

Rank, among children's most common fears, of being home alone: 1

Number of nightmares the average adult has in a year: 1

AMBITIONS

Percentage of Americans who say they want to live to 100: 49

Percentage of Americans who say they want their boss's job: 29

Percentage of female executives who say that wearing perfume helps a woman's career: 36

Percentage change, since 1965, in the number of young married couples with children: +10

In the number of young married couples without children: +82

Number of people who took a Dale Carnegie course in 1985: 118,461

Number of people in the world who speak Esperanto: 50,000

Number of people who attended the International Conference on Spelling Reform held in England in 1985: 17

ANACHRONISMS

Number of colonies in the world: 42

Leper population of the Americas: 320,000

Cases of bubonic plague reported in the United States in 1985: 17

Butler schools in the United States: 1

Nanny schools: 19

Number of crossbows in Britain: 250,000

Rank of national and local Miss America pageants among all sources of college scholarship money for women: 1

Percentage of diplomas that are printed on sheepskin: 3

Percentage of U.S. households that pay their bills exclusively in cash: 12

Number of American draft resisters still living in Canada: 10,000

Number of Americans who live on communes: 40,000

Estimated number of pirate attacks at sea since 1984: 83

Members of the Flat Earth Research Society: 2,800

ANOMALIES

Rank of "The Cosby Show," in popularity, among all shows on South African TV: 1

Number of blacks among the five Americans most admired by teenagers: 2

Rank of Ronald Reagan, among all foreign leaders, in popularity among the French: 1

Members of the Abraham Lincoln Association: 425

Members of the Calvin Coolidge Memorial Foundation: 650

Rank of Main among the most common street names in America: 32

Rank of Park: 1

Number of new products test-marketed in New York City in the last year: 198

In Peoria: 69

Copies of *Penthouse* and *Playboy* sold, per 1,000 residents, in Des Moines: 160

In New York City: 42

Quarts of ice cream eaten by the average Southerner each year: 12

By the average New Englander: 23

Percentage of doctors who smoke: 17

Weight of the average male bear in Alaska (in pounds): 250

In Pennsylvania: 487

APPEARANCES

Percentage of American men who acknowledge that they wear uncomfortable shoes because they look good: 20

Percentage of American women who acknowledge that they wear uncomfortable shoes because they look good: 45

Percentage of Americans who think they look younger than they are: 57

Total man-hours spent mowing lawns in the United States each year: 2,220,000,000

Cost of a car wash at Steve's Detailing in New York City: $155

Amount of laundry an average American family of four washes in a year (in tons): 1

Pieces of luggage Tatum O'Neal brought with her when she moved in with John McEnroe: 22

Pairs of sunglasses owned by Jack Nicholson: 15

Nehru jackets owned by Sammy Davis, Jr.: 6

Percentage of American astronauts who have experienced motion sickness in space: 48

Percentage of those who have publicly discussed it: 0

Appetites

Pounds of food consumed by the average American each year: 1,417

Pounds of chemical additives: 9

Number of Americans who drink Coca-Cola for breakfast: 965,000

Percentage of girls 13 to 18 years old who say they have symptoms of anorexia nervosa: 9

Percentage of American men who say they enjoy sex more than money: 47

Percentage of American women who say this: 26

Rank of cruise control among options that new-car buyers desire most: 1

Rank of Saudi Arabia, Qatar, and the United Arab Emirates, among all nations, in per capita military expenditures: 1, 2, 3

Percentage of international arms exports to the Third World that goes to African nations: 17

Percentage of federal income tax paid by individuals in 1981 that went to military programs: 45.5

Percentage in 1986: 51.4

Percentage of Brazilians who suffer from malnutrition: 65

Pounds of pasta that the average American ate in 1975: 9.7

In 1985: 12.3

Portion of ice cream sold in 1976 that was vanilla: ½

Today: ⅓

Ounces of snail eggs Parisians ate in 1985: 400

Rank of peanut M&M's among all candies sold at New York City subway newsstands: 1

Reported cases of people bitten by rats in New York City in 1985: 311

Reported cases of people bitten by other people: 1,519

BARGAINS

Amount General Dynamics was fined by the Pentagon in 1985 for improper activities: $676,283.80

Value of Pentagon contracts awarded to General Dynamics in 1985: $7,100,000,000

Average penalty levied by the Occupational Safety and Health Administration for a "serious" violation of safety regulations in 1985: $195

Number of Americans who declared over $200,000 in income and paid no federal taxes in 1983: 579

Number of the top six military contractors that have paid less than 3 percent in federal income taxes annually since 1981: 5

Cost of the Vietnam War in 1983 dollars: $430,200,000,000

Cost of the American Civil War: $36,900,000,000

Cost of planting the average 15-by-20-foot vegetable garden: $31

Value of that garden's yield of vegetables: $250

Cost of leasing one New York State sugar maple tree for a single sap season: $29

Cost of making a cubic foot of snow: 3¢

Purchase price of a parking space in New York City's first condominium garage: $29,000

Monthly maintenance fee for a space in that garage: $145.67

Price of a week's stay for a family of four at the Solair Nudist Park in Massachusetts: $260

BLACK AND WHITE

Percentage of all coronary bypass operations that are performed on whites: 97

Number of the 68 U.S. convicts executed since 1977 whose victims were not white: 7

Percentage increase in marriages between blacks and whites since 1977: 33

Percentage of Americans who believe there should be a law against interracial marriage: 27

Percentage of Americans who say that blacks "should not push themselves where they are not wanted": 58

Percentage of black Americans with college degrees who work for government: 64

Portion of black mayors who head cities that don't have black majorities: 1/3

Percentage of black baseball players in leadership positions (catcher, shortstop, second base): 15

Percentage of whites who say that college athletes should be paid: 15

Percentage of blacks who say this: 41

Percentage of whites who say that peacetime military service is "a very important obligation": 31

Percentage of blacks who say this: 45

CHIMERA

Percentage of Americans who believe that crime is increasing in the area in which they live: 53

Percentage change in the U.S. crime rate since 1981: − 16

Estimated percentage of missing American children who have been abducted by strangers: 1

Number of the 3,010 terrorist attacks worldwide in 1985 that involved Americans: 99

U.S. military ground personnel in Central America: 11,800

Cuban military ground personnel in Central America: 3,000

Portion of America's annual rainfall that falls in April: $1/12$

Forgeries discovered since 1980 in the collection of New York's Metropolitan Museum of Art: 50

Value of counterfeit products seized in the United States in 1985: $40,606,929

Percentage of newspaper stories that quote an unnamed source: 33

Percentage of elementary schoolchildren characterized as hyperactive by their teachers: 85

Number of murders the average child has seen on television by the age of 16: 18,000

Percentage of New York City police officers who fired their guns in the line of duty in 1985: 0.95

COMEBACKS

Black bear population of New Jersey in 1970: 12

In 1986: 100

Number of bald eagles counted in the United States in 1979: 9,815

In 1985: 10,807

New episodes of "Perry Mason" produced since 1985: 4

Percentage of college students who attended a religious service in 1985: 84.9

Percentage increase in the number of job applications received by the CIA in 1985: 50

Percentage increase, since 1984, in the number of job inquiries to the Peace Corps: 22

Number of "tabs" of LSD seized by the government in 1985: 3,590,979

COMFORTS

Total hours of television watched in American households in 1985: 224,372,599,000

Number of laughs the average person has in a day: 15

Rank of Nevada, the District of Columbia, and New Hampshire in per capita alcohol consumption: 1, 2, 3

Price of a fully equipped "terrorist-proof" Mercedes 500 at Washington's Counter Spy Shop: $208,000

Percentage of Russian soldiers that God will kill at the end of the world, according to Jerry Falwell: 83

Portion of the top 250 industrial companies that had "golden parachute" plans for their executives in 1982: ⅕

Portion that have them today: ⅓

Cost of raising a medium-size dog to the age of 11: $5,902

Number of U.S. pet cemeteries: 400

Average price of a pheasant at Lobel's butcher shop in New York: $32.50

Amount spent by Americans annually for packaged cookies: $3,900,000,000

Amount spent annually on pornography: $8,000,000,000

Number of romance novels published each month in the United States in 1985: 120

Rank of "The Cosby Show," "Miami Vice," and "Dallas" among prime-time programs most frequently taped at home: 1, 2, 3

Rank of Marcus Welby, Hawkeye Pierce, and Donald Westphall among TV doctors that Americans would go to if they existed: 1, 2, 3

Percentage of Americans who often feel they did something exactly right: 55

Who often sing, hum, or whistle: 48

Percentage of Americans who believe heaven exists: 84

Percentage who expect to enter therein: 66

CONDITIONS

Number of refugees currently seeking asylum, worldwide: 10,000,000

Portion of the world's population living under military-controlled governments: 1/5

Percentage of black children who live below the poverty line: 46.7

Percentage of Vietnam veterans who have suffered from post-traumatic stress disorder: 25

Number of mental disorders recognized by the American Psychiatric Association in 1952: 110

Today: 210

Percentage of American fifth-graders who report being in love: 39

Percentage of Americans who say they find life dull: 6

CONFIRMATIONS

Estimated percentage of professional boxers who suffer brain damage: 87

Number of firearms, per capita, in Detroit: 0.8

Percentage of Americans who own running shoes but don't run: 70

Rank of shopping for clothes among American women's favorite shopping trips: 1

Rank of shopping for a car among American men's: 1

Percentage of the board members of Fortune 1000 companies that are white and male: 92.8

Percentage of President Reagan's time that has been spent on vacation or at Camp David: 24

Percentage of President Carter's time that was spent this way: 10

Percentage of firefighters' meals that are interrupted: 60

Cups of tea the average Briton drinks each day: 3.77

Rank of Italy, among all nations, in per capita pasta consumption: 1

Percentage of the U.S. population that is Asian-American: 1.6

Percentage of the 1986 freshman class at MIT that is Asian-American: 18

Professional Ping-Pong players in China: 600

Average weight of a Chinese man's testicles (in grams): 19.01

Of a Dane's: 42

Rank of Rover, Spot, and Max among the most popular names for American dogs: 1, 2, 3

CONSEQUENCES

Percentage decrease in a household's television viewing after the acquisition of a personal computer: 40

Estimated number of defense industry jobs that would be lost in the event of a nuclear freeze: 350,000

Estimated amount of money that a nuclear freeze would save the U.S. between now and the year 2000: $400,000,000,000

Portion by which a baseball is compressed when hit squarely: ¼

Chances that an abused woman who does not notify the police will be assaulted again within the next six months: 2 in 5

Average percentage change in a woman's standard of living in the year after a divorce: − 73

Average percentage change in a man's standard of living in the year after a divorce: + 43

Percentage of executive men who are single or divorced: 4

Percentage of executive women who are single or divorced: 52

Percentage increase since 1980 in the number of Houston businesses filing for bankruptcy each month: 368

Tax revenues lost by Oklahoma each time the price of a barrel of oil drops a dollar: $11,000,000

Number of Oklahomans who contributed $10,000 or more to the Republican Party in 1981: 140

In 1986: 15

Percentage increase in Atlantic City's crime rate since gambling was legalized there: 275

CONVERSIONS

Number of South Africans whose race was legally reclassified in 1985: 1,167

Percentage of Republicans in 1955 who were white Southerners: 10

Percentage who are today: 33

Latin American countries in which military governments have been replaced with civilian ones since 1979: 10

Private enterprises licensed in China: 8,740,000

Price of a founding membership in the Beijing International Golf Club: $15,000

Value of British government assets that Prime Minister Thatcher has sold since 1979: $20,000,000,000

Portion of hospital beds in American cities that were in public hospitals in 1950: $\frac{1}{3}$

In 1985: $\frac{1}{7}$

Number of privately operated prisons in the United States: 30

Number of states in which parolees and probationers can be required to help pay for their own supervision: 23

Percentage of total movie industry revenues derived from theatrical distribution in 1978: 80

In 1985: 43

Number of seats on an American Airlines 727-200 before deregulation: 129

Number today: 150

CROSSOVERS

Number of sex-change operations performed in the United States each year: 225

Percentage of condoms that were bought by women in 1975: 15

Percentage today: 40

Percentage of Kellogg's Frosted Flakes eaters who are adults: 46

Percentage of Iowans who say they listen "fairly often" to soul music: 13

Percentage of country music records bought by minorities: 3

Percentage of Pentagon officers who retired in 1983 and 1984 to work for defense contractors on the same project they worked on at the Pentagon: 20

Number of New York City police officers who are members of the Screen Actors Guild: 350

Percentage of American Protestants who say that "All in the Family" is the best sitcom ever: 5

Percentage of American Jews who say this: 15

Percentage of Jewish households in the United States that have Christmas trees: 9

CUSTOMS

Pool halls and bowling alleys per 100,000 residents in Chicago: 3.56

In Seattle: 7.15

Percentage of families in Iowa in which the wife does the laundry: 87

In which the husband takes out the trash: 55

Percentage of Berkeley's trash that is recycled: 16

Minimum number of paid vacation days, after one year of service, for workers in France: 25

For workers in the Soviet Union: 15

Paid vacation days for the average American worker: 8.7

Gang-related homicides in New York City in 1985: 5

In Los Angeles: 149

Number of the 68 executions in the United States since 1977 that occurred outside the South: 5

Average number of wives burned to death by their husbands each day in Delhi, India: 2

Percentage of the Americans dying in 1970 who were cremated: 5

Percentage in 1985: 14

Number of abortions for every 100 live births in the United States: 42

In the Soviet Union: 208

Percentage of babies born to unmarried white women under 25 that are given up for adoption: 8

Percentage born to unmarried black women: 1

Percentage of women who return to work within six months of giving birth: 63

Percentage of American families headed by a single parent: 26

Articles of clothing bought by the average woman in a year: 52

Bought by the average man: 33

Percentage of American car owners who keep sunglasses in their glove compartments: 23

DAYDREAMS

Percentage of Americans who say they daydream about being rich: 52

About being elected to public office: 6

Number of sexual fantasies the average person has in a day: 7

Percentage of *Vogue* readers who wear a size 12 or larger: 49

Percentage of Jeeps sold in 1986 that were bought by people living in urban or suburban areas: 60

Number of Americans holding reservations with Pan Am for a trip to the moon: 92,002

Number of European monarchs to whom the Murdoch press says Ronald Reagan is related: 9

Number of Vietnamese and Russians killed on screen in *Rambo*: 75

Number of Americans: 1

Estimated amount of contributions to the Nicaraguan contras from private American groups and citizens in 1985: $20,000,000

Number of people who have applied for the job of executioner in New Jersey: 75

Percentage of baseball players signed to professional contracts who never appear in a major-league game: 90

Percentage of men who say their biggest sports thrill would be to get the winning hit in the World Series: 32

Percentage of women who say this: 37

Percentage of teenagers' favorite songs that they say are about sex, violence, satanism, or drugs: 7

Percentage they say are about love: 26

Deliveries

Percentage of children born in 1961 who were firstborns: 25.8

Percentage today: 43

Average number of jokes in a 40-minute Henny Youngman monologue: 245

Percentage of U.S. oil imports today that come from Mexico, Canada, and Britain: 33

Percentage that come from Arab countries: 21

Tons of cargo handled at the Port of New York and New Jersey in 1985: 54,722,500

At the Port of Los Angeles: 16,971,000

Percentage of the marijuana smoked in America that is imported: 45

Percentage of Americans who say they have had a pizza delivered in the last three months: 40

Pieces of mail the average person receives in a year: 598

George Bernard Shaw's lifetime postage bill (at today's rates): $50,000

DISAPPEARANCES

Acres of the world's tropical rain forests cleared every minute: 53

Pieces of mail that end up at the dead-letter office each year: 75,100,000

Amount the U.S. government spent on paper shredders in 1985: $4,300,000

Number of senior Soviet officials who have been removed since Gorbachev came to power: 141

Number of Chinese Communist Party officials who have been forced to retire since 1981: 900,000

Number of Americans declared missing in action during Vietnam War: 2,435

During World War II: 78,751

Percentage of the 90,000 Latin Americans "disappeared" since 1963 who were Guatemalan: 39

Coverage of South Africa on ABC's "World News Tonight" in the month before Pretoria's November 1985 media ban (in minutes): 10.8

In the month after the ban: 3.2

Number of new American plays and adaptations that appeared on Broadway in 1959: 27

In 1985: 10

Number of radio stations with a disco format today: 0

Estimated number of weathervanes reported stolen in Maine in the last year: 80

Percentage decrease in the patient population of U.S. psychiatric hospitals since 1955: 79

Copies of *Catcher in the Rye* that have been checked out of public libraries in Chicago and never returned: 7,500

DISPARITIES

Budget per episode of "Miami Vice": $1,500,000

Annual budget of the Miami vice squad: $1,161,741

Number of guests at the wedding of Ronald Reagan's daughter Patti: 134

Number of police officers and Secret Service agents: 180

U.S. foreign aid in 1985: $12,327,000,000

Interest payments on the federal debt that were made to foreigners in 1985: $21,500,000,000

Cost to consumers of "protecting" one job in the automobile industry via import restrictions: $160,000

Average yearly wages of an American auto worker: $24,960

Annual earnings, including overtime, of a Carnegie Hall stagehand: $70,000

Percentage of black high school graduates under 25 who are unemployed: 23.6

Percentage of white high school dropouts under 25 who are unemployed: 16.3

Percentage of executive men who have had a child by age 40: 90

Percentage of executive women who have had a child by age 40: 35

Percentage change in the buying power of the average Social Security check since 1970: +48

Of the average Aid to Families with Dependent Children check: −31

Federal tax revenues lost as a result of homeowner deductions in 1985: $43,600,000,000

Amount spent for federal housing programs in 1985: $12,300,000,000

Percentage change in the number of FAA-certified airlines since deregulation: +150

Percentage change in the number of FAA inspectors since deregulation: +2

Amount spent annually in the United States on private security forces: $21,700,000,000

On public police forces: $13,800,000,000

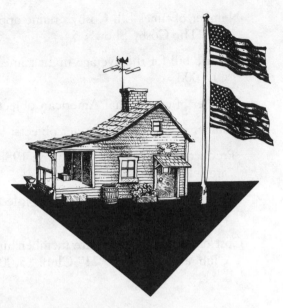

DISPLAYS

Average number of times that a man cries in a month: 1.4

Number of times that a woman cries: 5.3

Percentage of motor vehicles with vanity plates in Illinois: 1.1

In California: 3.6

Percentage increase in the number of BMWs sold in the United States since 1975: 350

Number of Rolls-Royces in the Soviet Union: 6

Cost of renting the *Queen Elizabeth 2* for an overnight "cruise to nowhere": $500,000

Percentage increase in sales of American flags in 1986: 15

Flag "desecrations" recorded by the FBI in 1985: 11

Number of pencils and index cards David Letterman tosses over his shoulder during an average show: 4

Number of times Bill Cosby's name appears in the credits for "The Cosby Show": 5

Electric bill for the average night game at Shea Stadium: $12,000

Number of operational American objects in space: 520

Number of operational Soviet objects: 948

"Product categories" for which the 1988 Olympic organizers are selling official sponsorships: 44

Corporate sponsors for the 1986 dogsled expedition to the North Pole: 65

Cost of an annual corporate membership in the Breakfast Club at New York's "21" Club: $5,000

DIVERSIONS

Rank of Alaska and Utah, among all states, in birth rate: 1, 2

Movie theaters in the United States: 18,000

In the Soviet Union: 151,280

Number of toys given away in boxes of Cracker Jack since 1912: 16,000,000,000

Weekly sales per square foot near the cash registers in the average supermarket: $22.80

Weekly sales per square foot elsewhere in the store: $7.76

Percentage of American men earning less than $5,000 a year who say they cheat on their wives: 16

Percentage of men earning $70,000 or more who say they cheat on their wives: 70

ENTHUSIASMS

People on the waiting list to see an execution in Florida: 215

Percentage of Americans who say they are "very likely" to become organ donors: 32

Percentage of Americans who say they are "very likely" to donate a "loved one's" organs: 70

Rank of tofu, liver, and yogurt among foods that Americans hate: 1, 2, 3

Number of Americans who have not been to the dentist in over a year: 122,000,000

Percentage of Americans who say they feel young for their age: 66

Number of Americans who play the accordion: 2,200,000

Number of Christian rock albums sold in 1985: 20,000,000

Percentage of Iowans who would like to be reincarnated as themselves: 64

Number of Ant Farms sold since their invention 30 years ago: 7,250,000

Price of a 1909 Honus Wagner baseball card: $32,000

Amount that Pat Paulsen has raised for his 1988 presidential campaign: $335

EPHEMERA

Industry estimate of the life span of an umbrella (in years): 1.5

Life span of an adult mayfly (in days): 1

Life span of a baseball in a major-league game (in pitches): 5

Cost per second of advertising time on "The Cosby Show": $12,700

Percentage of supermarket buying decisions that are made in the store: 65

Mary Lou Retton's "performer Q" popularity and recognition rating in 1984: 53

Today: 25

Number of pornographic videocassettes released each week: 100

Average length of sexual intercourse for humans (in minutes): 2

For chimpanzees (in seconds): 7

EQUIVALENCES

Number of videocassettes rented in 1985: 1,200,000,000

Number of books checked out from public libraries: 1,197,000,000

Total annual expenditures of U.S. corporations on employee-education programs: $60,000,000,000

Total annual expenditures of U.S. four-year public and private colleges and universities: $60,000,000,000

Amount Mexico has borrowed abroad since 1974: $97,000,000,000

Value of investments and deposits made abroad by Mexicans since 1974: $90,300,000,000

Amount the government reimbursed Ed Meese for legal expenses incurred in his 1985 Ethics Act inquiry: $472,190

Federal funds allocated for legal aid to the poor in Delaware that year: $533,510

Average percentage of their income that Americans earning $200,000 or more will pay under the new tax bill: 22

Average percentage they pay today: 22

Diameter of TV's Wheel of Fortune: 8'6"

Height of basketball player Manute Bol: 7'6¾"

Ratio of physicians to inhabitants of the United States: 1 to 549

Ratio of prison inmates to inhabitants: 1 to 497

EXITS AND ENTRANCES

Rank of August, among all months, in the number of Americans who die in auto accidents: 1

Rank of August in the number of Americans born: 1

Percentage increase since 1975 in births by cesarean section in the United States: 132

Percentage of visits to doctors' offices that last less than 11 minutes: 45

Number of animals freed from U.S. research laboratories by animal-rights groups in 1985: 2,167

Average number of parrots smuggled into the United States from Mexico every day: 137

Percentage of Americans who say they have made changes in their lives to "get out of the rat race": 40

Number of Americans who emigrate each year: 100,000

Portion of legal immigrants to the United States since 1930 who were women or children: 2/3

Percentage increase in foreign investment in American companies since 1973: 790

Portion of all goods sold in the United States today that are imported: 1/4

Number of new products introduced in the United States in 1985: 12,500

Percentage of men between the ages of 55 and 59 who were retired in 1970: 10.5

Who are retired today: 20

Number of homosexuals discharged from the U.S. military in 1985: 1,800

Number of Soviet embassy officials expelled by host governments in 1986: 94

Number of Americans who drown each year: 5,500

Price of a contract killing in the Bronx: $5,000

EXPOSURES

Percentage of American men who say they sleep in the nude: 19

Percentage of women: 6

Americans arrested for spying on the United States from 1965 to 1975: 7

Since 1975: 50

Percentage of lawyers who advertise: 17

Percentage of Americans in 1985 who didn't recognize Mr. Clean: 7

Who didn't recognize George Bush: 44

Chances that an American has appeared on TV: 1 in 4

Percentage of all snapshots taken in America in 1984 that were snapped at Disneyland, Disney World, or Epcot Center: 3.6

Percentage of liberals who say they've gone skinny-dipping: 28

Percentage of conservatives: 15

Gallons of suntan lotion and oil used by Americans in 1985: 1,300,000

Gallons of calamine lotion sold in 1985: 7,100,427

Number of Americans who freeze to death each year: 500

FAÇADES

Number of trench coats owned by Morley Safer: 5

Number of firms listed in the 1978 edition of the *Directory of Personal Image Consultants*: 36

In the 1986 edition: 364

Amount that South Africa spends annually for lobbyists in the United States: $2,000,000

Number of U.S. Air Force personnel assigned to investigations and counterintelligence: 1,423

Number assigned to public affairs: 1,862

Medals awarded by the military for action in Grenada: 9,754

Amount spent by the U.S. government on advertising in 1985: $259,000,000

Amount spent by Coca-Cola: $390,000,000

Number of U.S. savings and loan companies that have added the word "bank" to their names since 1984: 116

Estimated number of Americans who have counterfeit diplomas or credentials: 500,000

Number of Americans who have surgery each year solely to improve their appearance: 720,000

Rank of Richard Nixon masks among the best-selling Halloween masks bought by adults: 1

FADS

Total sales of products tied to the most recent pass of Halley's Comet: $500,000,000

Gallons of urine analyzed for evidence of illegal drug use in 1985: 1,190

Percentage change in the number of libel suits filed since 1984: −30

Percentage increase in sales of GI Joe toys since 1982: 177

Number of college courses offered on the Vietnam War in 1980: 58

Today: 157

Number of colleges and universities offering courses in "men's studies" in 1984: 30

Today: 100

Cost of a week's tuition for two parents at Philadelphia's Better Baby Institute: $980

Cost of a week at camp in Maine for a Cabbage Patch doll: $150

Season tickets to spring training sold by the Los Angeles Dodgers in 1977: 630

In 1986: 3,279

Percentage change in sales of tennis rackets since 1977: −70

Number of the three best-selling automobiles in 1985 that were pickup trucks: 2

New game shows offered to TV stations in 1985: 17

In 1986: 31

Number of "big band" radio stations in 1982: 388

Today: 934

Rank of "Grandma Got Run Over by a Reindeer," among all Christmas singles, in sales in 1985: 1

FREAKS AND WONDERS

Number of the five all-time highest grossing films that were made by Steven Spielberg, George Lucas, or both: 5

Most books on the *New York Times* best-seller lists at one time edited by a single editor (Michael Korda): 7

Rank of the southeast corner of 59th and Lexington among the world's most crowded streetcorners: 1

Highest price paid for a cow at auction: $1,300,000

Greatest pumpkin ever grown (in pounds): 671

Longest recorded flight by a chicken: 302' 8"

FRUITS AND VEGETABLES

Percentage change since 1971 in per capita consumption of green peas: −27

In the consumption of broccoli: +160

Items in the average grocery store's produce section in 1976: 50

Today: 200

Average amount a household spends on vegetables each week: $1.74

Percentage of backyard gardeners who grow tomatoes: 94

Who grow parsnips: 5

Pounds of apples eaten by the average American in 1910: 54

In 1985: 17

Percentage increase in the number of vegetarians in England since 1983: 30

Percentage of third-graders in Oklahoma who say they chew tobacco: 7

Number of write-in votes in the 1985 Boise, Idaho, mayoral election cast for Mr. Potato Head: 4

GRAND TOTALS

Number of bird species that have been sighted in Central Park since its opening in 1858: 259

Grains of sand on the surface of New York's Jones Beach: 2,230,000,000,000

Number of beer cans manufactured since they were introduced in 1935: 610,000,000,000

Total horsepower at the 1986 Indianapolis 500: 24,000

At the 1986 Kentucky Derby: 800

Number of pigs kept as pets in residential areas of the United States: 100

Tons of barbecue sold on July 4, 1986, at Piggie Park Restaurant in Columbia, South Carolina: 18

Possible games of chess: 25×10^{115}

Estimated number of scientific and technical articles published each day, worldwide: 17,000

Number of dreams the average person has in a year: 1,460

Number of commercials for Coca-Cola that the average American sees in a year: 69

Estimated number of interviews conducted by opinion pollsters in the United States each year: 20,000,000

Largest number of footnotes in a law review article: 3,340

Combined value of all the currency and coin in circulation in the United States: $199,000,000,000

Combined net worth of the 400 richest Americans: $156,000,000,000,000

Number of elementary particles in the observable universe: 100,000,000,000,000,000,000,000,000,000,000,000,000,000,000,000,000,000,000,000,000,000,000,000,000,000,000,000,000,000,000,000

GUNS AND BUTTER

Pounds of butter that can be bought (at $2.12 a lb.) for the cost of an M16 rifle: 263

HEGEMONY (American)

Number of nations where "Dallas" appears on television: 98

Price of a Jane Fonda workout videocassette on the black market in Moscow: $370

Copies of *Iacocca* sold in Japan: 400,000

Number of "American-style" homes built in Japan in 1985: 26,000

Percentage of Japan's red-pepper-sauce market held by Tabasco: 99

Percentage of the U.S. pencil market supplied by domestic manufacturers: 93

Portion of the world's exports in 1985 that was imported by the United States: 1/5

Percentage of programs broadcast in Nicaragua that are made in the United States: 30

Attacks made on the United States in speeches at the 1980 conference of nonaligned nations, in Havana: 14

Number made at the 1986 conference, in Harare, Zimbabwe: 66

Number of students in the United States who are studying Russian: 25,000

Students in the Soviet Union who are studying English: 4,000,000

Number of Fabergé Imperial eggs owned by the Kremlin: 10

Number owned by Malcolm Forbes: 11

Percentage of Japanese who say that Disneyland brings "the most happiness into their lives": 50

"Rambos" in the Washington, D.C., phone book: 3

HEGEMONY (Japanese)

Robot population of the United States: 25,000

Of Japan: 75,000

Hours that Japanese teenagers spend each week in class or studying: 59

Soviet teenagers: 51.5

American teenagers: 38

Percentage of Japan's machine tools that are over ten years old: 39

Percentage of America's machine tools that are: 69

Number of Japanese cars imported into the United States in 1985: 2,527,479

Vice versa: 1,290

Rank of vehicles, audio and video recorders, and office equipment among Japan's leading exports to the United States in 1984: 1, 2, 3

Rank of corn, soybeans, and coal among the United States' leading exports to Japan in 1984: 1, 2, 3

Number of the ten largest international banks that are Japanese: 6

Amount of capital that Japan invests abroad each month: $7,000,000,000

HEGEMONY (Soviet)

Total hours that the Russian population spends waiting in line for food each year: 37,000,000,000

Life expectancy of a Soviet man born in 1966 (in years): 66

In 1979: 62

Percentage change in Warsaw Pact manpower since 1983: +1.3

In NATO manpower: +7.3

Foreign-aid budget of the Soviet Union in 1978: $3,500,000,000

In 1985: $2,500,000,000

Ratio of students to personal computer in public schools in the United States: 41 to 1

In the Soviet Union: 22,500 to 1

Number of photocopies that the Lenin Library in Moscow allows visitors to make each day: 2,000

Portion of the Soviet Union's urban population that shares a kitchen and bathroom with another family: 1/6

HOSTS AND GUESTS

Percentage of requests by Poles for asylum in the United States that were granted in 1985: 33

Percentage of requests by Salvadorans: 2

Percentage of requests by Nicaraguans: 10

Number of foreigners apprehended for illegally crossing the U.S. border in 1985: 1,348,749

Percentage increase, since 1970, in the number of Americans 18 to 34 years old living with their parents: 52

Percentage of Americans over 60 who live with a younger relative: 6.3

Percentage of Japanese over 60 who do: 70

Rank of Los Angeles, among all U.S. cities, in the number of homeless people: 1

Average number of South Africans detained every hour since the government declared a state of emergency: 8

Percentage of Thai women between the ages of 15 and 30 who are prostitutes: 10

Estimated number of cockroaches in the Pentagon: 2,000,000

ICONOCLASTS

Percentage of Americans who refuse to take part in market research surveys: 38

Number of Americans who have requested that their names be removed from direct-mail marketing lists: 496,000

Number of U.S. university scientists who have pledged to refuse Star Wars research funds: 3,800

Number of Finnish women who have pledged not to have children until Finland bans nuclear power: 4,000

Percentage of Americans who say they would not accept a job if a lie detector test were required: 55

Percentage of Iowans who say they didn't try to see Halley's Comet: 74

Number of votes that Donald Duck received in the 1985 Swedish parliamentary elections: 291

IDEALS

Barbie's measurements (if she were life-size): 39–23–33

Weight of the average female fashion model in 1970 (in pounds): 112

Today: 122

Percentage of American families composed of a father who works, a mother who doesn't, and two children: 4

Rank of steak and potatoes among Americans' favorite foods: 1, 2

Number of holes-in-one that American golfers claim to hit every day: 119

IMPORTS AND EXPORTS

Portion of Bolivia's $1.1 billion in export earnings in 1985 accounted for by cocaine: ⅖

Amount that Latin American countries earned on their exports in 1985: $125,000,000,000

Amount they paid in principal and interest on their debts: $55,000,000,000

Percentage of Japan's gross national product accounted for by export earnings: 17

Percentage of South Korea's gross national product that is: 33

Percentage of legal immigrants to the United States in 1985 that came from Asia: 46

Percentage increase in containers of cargo shipped between Asia and the United States since 1983: 62

Chances that an American doctor graduated from a foreign medical school: 1 in 5

Percentage of Ph.D. graduates of U.S. engineering schools who are foreigners: 59

INFRASTRUCTURE

Potholes in the United States: 55,961,000

Cavities in the teeth of the average 15-year-old: 8

Percentage of international telephone conversations that are conducted in English: 85

Percentage of U.S. college freshmen who are enrolled in a remedial math class: 25

Number of employees it takes to answer a letter received by the Secretary of Health and Human Services: 55

Number of IMF-member countries operating with a deficit: 86

Number operating with a surplus: 35

Percentage of Japan's corporate R&D in 1984 that was funded by the government: 1.8

Percentage of the United States': 32.3

Government estimate of the value of the untaxed U.S. underground economy: $9,000,000,000

Percentage of the nation's electrical output used for cooling purposes: 15

Percentage of all water used by humans that is used for irrigation: 80

Portion of the world's population that cooks with wood or charcoal: ½

Percentage of refrigerators in American households that are either white or almond: 90

Percentage of American women who wear the wrong size bra: 75

Percentage of Americans who say they don't know how they could get along without Scotch tape: 46

IN KIND

Pounds of frozen chicken that Peru exported to the Soviet Union in 1985 to help pay back a loan: 1,860,432

Tons of hair that Poland exports annually to West Germany in exchange for barber equipment: 100

Number of Pontiacs in Pontiac, Michigan: 3,723

Number of tombstones in Tombstone, Arizona: 792

INNOCENCE AND EXPERIENCE

Percentage of Americans who say the United States has never used nuclear weapons in a war: 11

Percentage of Americans who never read books: 45

Rejection rate of applicants for the 1985 kindergarten class at Manhattan's Trinity Episcopal School: 85

For the 1985 entering class at Stanford: 86

Percentage of Soviet children who believe a nuclear war can be prevented: 92

Percentage of American children who believe this: 65

Percentage of fifth-graders who say they think a lot about hunger and poverty in the United States: 52

Percentage of ninth-graders who say this: 31

Percentage of black American children who do not live with either parent: 8

Chances that a first-time bride in Kentucky is a teen-ager: 1 in 2

Percentage of female college students who say they have been raped: 16

Percentage of those who say the rapist was someone they were dating: 57

Chances that a man has spent a night in jail: 1 in 5

Number of Cocaine Anonymous meetings held each week in Los Angeles: 75

Number held there three years ago: 6

Portion of American adults who don't drink: ⅓

Armed robberies in the history of Iceland: 1

IN STEP

Percentage of the funds the Pentagon has requested since 1981 that Congress has appropriated: 92.1

Number of White House requests for arms sales to a foreign country that Congress has rejected: 1

Percentage of Americans who say they don't know anyone who doesn't like Jell-O: 55

Rank of Alaska, among all states, in the percentage of people who walk to work: 1

Pairs of toe shoes the New York City Ballet orders for principal dancer Suzanne Farrell each season: 350

Percentage of women executives with MBAs who say their pregnancies were planned: 93.8

Percentage of fathers who were in the delivery room when their children were born in 1973: 27

Today: 79

Percentage increase, since 1973, in three- and four-year-olds attending nursery school: 91

Percentage of Fortune 500 companies that tested employees and job applicants for illegal drug use in 1982: 10

Percentage that test today: 30

Number of states that have passed stricter drunk-driving laws since 1982: 45

Number of states that raised high school graduation requirements since 1980: 40

Number of high school marching bands that ordered the sheet music for "Barbara Ann" in 1986: 2,600

ISOLATIONISTS

Percentage of Americans who say the United States should not send troops if an Arab country overruns Israel: 53

Who say the United States should not send troops if Nicaragua invades Honduras: 59

Portion of the American population that has never flown in an airplane: ⅓

Percentage of Americans who never go to the movies: 39

Chances that an American has never eaten a bagel: 4 in 5

Percentage of the 2,000 referendums on water fluoridation held since 1950 that have been voted down: 60

Portion of American households made up of a single person in 1955: ⅒

Today: ¼

Number of days each year that TV broadcasting is
   prohibited in Iceland: 52

JOURNEYS

Number of South Africans who emigrate each day: 40

Number of Ethiopians who arrive in Somalia each day:
   1,000

Number of Jews permitted to emigrate from the Soviet
   Union in 1979: 51,320

In 1985: 1,140

Number of Haitians intercepted trying to enter the United
   States in the nine months before "Baby Doc" Duvalier
   fled to France: 1,601

Number intercepted in the first nine months after he fled:
   2,859

Number of cruise ships scheduled to make stops at Cuban ports in 1986: 17

Number of Americans who commute from a suburb to a city to go to work: 13,900,000

Who commute from one suburb to another: 26,900,000

Estimated number of miles walked on the job in a year by a factory worker: 2,227

By a housewife: 1,037

Percentage of Americans who have visited Yellowstone National Park: 30

Number of people who have barreled over Niagara Falls and survived: 8

Cab fare from New York to Los Angeles: $5,500

JUDGMENTS

Percentage of Americans who say the "bad effects" of nuclear energy outweigh the good: 38

Who say the bad effects of credit cards outweigh the good: 46

Percentage of Iowans who think music videos are among the "least useful changes" in modern life: 67

Percentage of Americans who rank Detroit as the nation's worst city: 64

Percentage of Costa Ricans who say that Nicaragua interferes too much in Costa Rica's internal affairs: 40

Percentage who say that the United States interferes too much: 50

Percentage of Americans who, in 1981, thought their chances of surviving a nuclear war were fifty-fifty: 32

Who think so today: 17

Percentage of Midwesterners who judge their chances of going to heaven as good to excellent: 69

Percentage of Americans who say they are "dissatisfied with the honesty and standards" of others: 63

Percentage of Americans who said in 1957 that an unmarried woman was "sick," "neurotic," or "immoral": 80

Percentage of Americans who say that being single today is "not a fully acceptable life-style": 38

Percentage of Americans who say television news portrays politicians too favorably: 46

Who say it portrays professional sports stars too favorably: 54

Percentage of libel cases in which juries rule against media defendants: 75

Percentage of those verdicts that are reversed on appeal: 60

Percentage of Americans who say the wheel is the greatest invention of all time: 11

Percentage who say the automobile is: 10

LABOR RELATIONS

Average percentage increase in the pay of nonunion workers in the last year: 4.2

In the pay of union workers: 2.5

Hours the average American worked each week in 1973: 40.6

In 1985: 47.3

Percentage of families living below the poverty line in which at least one member is employed: 60

Percentage of unemployed Americans who receive no unemployment benefits: 75

Estimated number of new computer programming jobs that will be created by 1995: 245,000

Number of secretarial jobs that will be created: 267,000

Percentage of fast-food workers who say they are satisfied with their jobs: 61

Percentage of new jobs created between 1978 and 1984 that pay less than $9,200 annually: 37

Percentage change in buying power of the minimum wage since 1981: −26

LACUNAE

Percentage of American sixth-graders who cannot locate the United States on a world map: 20

Percentage of American 13-year-olds who think it is illegal to start a third political party: 58

Percentage of high school students who believe the President can declare a law unconstitutional: 49

Percentage of Americans who believe the accused are guilty until proven innocent: 50

Percentage of American high school seniors who identify Israel as an Arab nation: 40

Percentage of Americans who know which side the United States supports in Nicaragua: 50

Percentage of Americans who cannot name a country "near the Pacific Ocean": 42

Percentage of Americans who don't know how long a meter is: 66

Percentage of Americans who don't know who William Rehnquist is: 71

LANDSCAPES

Square yards of park per inhabitant in Paris: 6

In New York: 18

In Washington, D.C.: 62

Percentage of land in the average American city taken up by roads and parking spaces: 40

Number of billboards that are in violation of the 1965 Highway Beautification Act: 171,579

Portion of the U.S. landmass owned by the federal government: ⅓

Acres of land purchased for national parks by the Reagan administration: 151,515

By the Carter administration: 419,492

Number of wild mustangs in the American West: 51,880

Number of one-room schoolhouses in Nebraska: 376

Percentage of trees in New Hampshire whose leaves turn red in the fall: 13

Percentage change in acres of forest in New York State since 1880: +287

Life span of a sidewalk tree in New York City (in years): 7

Tulip bulbs planted along Park Avenue in New York City each year: 90,000

Number of different plants identified in inner-city Cleveland: 400

Total acres in the United States that are occupied by shopping centers and malls: 59,129

By vegetable gardens: 1,300,000

LIAISONS

Chances that a female graduate student in psychology has had sex with one of her professors: 1 in 6

Number of Americans carried to term by surrogate mothers: 500

Average duration of an American marriage (in years): 9.4

Chances that a child born out of wedlock was deliberately conceived: 1 in 5

Chances that a child born to a married couple was deliberately conceived: 3 in 5

Number of children's shows based on toys in 1983: 14

Today: 62

Number of corporate mergers per business day in 1986: 12

Percentage increase in joint ventures between the United States and Japan since 1980: 100

Value of bank loans to the East German government guaranteed by West Germany in 1984: $730,000,000

Estimated value of Israeli arms sales to Latin American nations in 1985: $200,000,000

Percentage of Nicaragua's exports that were bought by Japan in 1979: 3

In 1985: 25

Number of the 173 private religious schools in Nicaragua that are subsidized by the government: 121

Number of academic conferences sponsored by the CIA in 1985: 70

Miles of runway the U.S. military has built in Honduras since 1983: 7.3

Number of racquetball courts it has built there: 1

LOST AND FOUND

Value of the items the Pentagon misplaced in 1984: $1,021,876,000

Value of the items it found: $1,013,697,000

Fingers lost in fireworks-related accidents in 1985: 38

Body fluids through perspiration per hour of exercise in hot weather (in ounces): 54

Estimated hours of work lost in the United States each year to alcoholism: 6,000,000,000

Estimated hours of work that are lost each year because of menstrual cramps: 576,000,000

Corpses found in the Harlem, Hudson, and East rivers in 1985: 85

Percentage decrease in the number of coffin manufacturers and distributors in the United States since 1967: 38

Percentage of American television viewers who correctly identify the brand advertised on the last commercial they saw: 7

Percentage of Americans too young to remember the Bicentennial: 25

The launching of Sputnik: 58

Life before television: 69

Estimated percentage of nuts that squirrels lose because they forget where they put them: 50

MAINSTAYS

Number of times Mick Jagger has appeared on the cover of *Rolling Stone:* 13

Portion of the New York City Ballet's ticket income derived from performances of *The Nutcracker:* ¼

Amount that La Mancha, Spain, is spending to restore its 30 remaining medieval and Renaissance windmills: $78,500

Number of recordings of "White Christmas" that have been sold since its release: 164,958,934

Number of times the Beatles' "Yesterday" has been broadcast since 1970: 4,600,000

Percentage of all money spent by American tourists in Britain in 1984 that was spent at Harrods: 6

Tons of strawberries eaten at Wimbledon each year: 15

Gallons of mint juleps drunk at the Kentucky Derby: 1,875

MALADIES

Percentage of Medicare funds that go to people with less than a year to live: 28

Percentage of American women who receive no prenatal care during the first three months of pregnancy: 24

Chances that an American woman had in 1960 of developing breast cancer in her lifetime: 1 in 17

Her chances today: 1 in 10

56

Percentage of Americans between the ages of 6 and 17 who cannot pass a basic fitness test: 64

Chances that an American adult is obese: 1 in 4

Chances that an American Indian will die before the age of 45: 1 in 3

Amount spent on health care in the United States in 1985: $425,000,000,000

Percentage of that paid by the government: 41

Percentage of the U.S. population under 65 that has no health insurance: 15

U.S. spending on health care in 1980, expressed as a percentage of the gross national product: 5.3

Today: 10.6

Number of hearings the Senate health committee has held on AIDS: 1

MANNERS

Rank of Mother's Day in the number of long-distance phone calls placed: 1

Number of times the average man sees his parents each year: 47

The average woman: 62

Percentage of cohabitating couples who were unwed in 1970: 1

In 1984: 4

Percentage of American women who use deodorant: 92

Of American men: 86

Bars of soap used by the average French person in a year: 2

Percentage of Chicago restaurant managers who say they allow their patrons to smoke cigarettes: 84

To nurse a child: 34

Percentage of adolescent boys who say they "hit or beat up another kid" in the past year: 64

Percentage of Americans who say birth-control information should be available on TV: 78

Number of sites on British roads marked to protect toads crossing during the mating season: 150

Percentage of the nuclear waste in the world's oceans that was dumped by Britain: 90

Percentage of doctors in 1980 who said patients should be told the truth about their cancer: 18

Percentage who say this today: 70

MARKETS

Price of a 0.5 cc unit of a Holstein bull's semen: $15–$75

Price of a 0.5 cc unit of human semen: $48

Average fee charged by a surrogate mother: $10,000

Market value of the labor performed annually by the average American housewife: $40,288.04

Fee for a lecture by Henry Kissinger: $20,000

Estimated world military expenditures for 1986: $850,000,000,000

Percentage by which prices for Nazi memorabilia appreciate annually: 20

Average percentage return on an investment in Old Master paintings in 1984: 16.3

In 1985: 4

Per diem price of a bodyguard in Canton, China: $3

In New York City: $250

Monthly earnings of China's top female fashion model: $70

Portion of the disposable income in the United States that is spent by homosexuals: 1/5

Average number of homes a buyer looks at before making a purchase: 13.6

Shelf space taken up by pet food in the average American supermarket (in linear feet): 240

By soup: 105

Campaign dollars spent for each vote cast in the 1984 election: $3.50

Value placed on a life by the Occupational Safety and Health Administration: $3,000,000

By the Federal Aviation Administration: $650,000

MEDIA

Rank of the grapevine among employees' leading sources of information about their company: 1

Estimated number of underground newspapers and magazines published in Poland: 250

Average number of newspapers and periodicals to which a Soviet family subscribes: 6

To which an American family subscribes: 3.3

Portion of the personal mail sent in 1985 that consisted of greeting cards: ½

American adults who read below the eighth-grade level: 36,000,000

Number of Russians who subscribe to *The New York Times*: 7

Percentage of the information collected by U.S. agencies that is acquired by technical means: 85

That is acquired by agents: 15

Number of people a satisfied car owner tells about his car: 8

Number of people a dissatisfied car owner tells about his: 22

MOVEMENTS

Number of blacks who left the South between 1980 and 1985: 470,000

Number who moved to the South: 528,000

Percentage increase in the number of blacks registered to vote in the South since 1982: 16.2

Value of the art and antiques exported from England in 1985: £792,826,000

Walking speed of the average American woman (in feet per minute): 256

Of the average man: 245

Average speed of the winner in the men's 5,000-meter race at the 1912 Olympics (in miles per hour): 12.74

At the 1984 Olympics: 14.22

Number of feet the geographic center of U.S. population moves to the west each day: 58

Number of feet it moves to the south: 29

MUTANTS

Number of insect and related species resistant to pesticides in 1970: 224

In 1984: 447

Number of patented life forms: 374

Number of four-leaf clover farms in the United States: 1

Annual percentage growth in the U.S. robot population: 44

Number of Americans who have been killed on the job by a robot: 2

MYSTERIES

Percentage of household burglaries in the United States that are solved: 9

Percentage of Americans who say they dream in color: 40

Who say they dream in black and white: 23

Number of Americans who have received new identities under the Federal Witness Security Program: 16,500

Number of U.S. government employees who have authority to classify documents as secret: 2,242,602

Percentage of women who believe in love at first sight: 57

Of men: 66

NOSTRUMS

Percentage of Americans who believe the Russians are our enemies because they are atheists: 37

Percentage of Americans who believe differences in social standing reflect what people have made of their opportunities: 72

OBSERVANCES

Wreaths delivered to Graceland on Elvis's birthday every year: 60

Books published in West Germany in honor of the 500th anniversary of Luther's birth: 120

In East Germany: 50

Copies of George Orwell's *1984* sold each day in the United States in January 1984: 27,700

Bottles of Scotch imported by the Ethiopian government to celebrate its tenth anniversary: 480,000

Number of countries whose independence day is in July: 15

Percentage of Iowans who say they have a hard time singing "The Star Spangled Banner": 40

Percentage of all bills passed by Congress in 1985 that established commemorative days, weeks, or months: 36

Percentage of federal district court judges appointed by President Carter who are millionaires: 4

Percentage appointed by President Reagan in his first term who are: 22.5

Percentage decrease in church attendance by American Protestants since 1958: 5

By American Catholics: 23

Rank of Mother's Day in the number of Americans eating out: 1

Number of times mail carriers were bitten by dogs in 1985: 6,312

ODDS

Chances of a White Christmas in New York: 1 in 4

In Minneapolis: 3 in 4

Chances that a male North Dakotan is an Elk: 1 in 10

Chances that an adult in the San Francisco Bay Area has completed *est* training: 1 in 69

Chances that a physician is an imposter: 1 in 50

Chances that a resident of Washington, D.C., is a lawyer: 1 in 25

Chances that a white, college-educated 25-year-old woman will marry: 1 in 2

Chances that a white, college-educated 35-year-old woman will marry: 1 in 18

Chances that a working woman earns more than her husband: 1 in 5

OMENS

Percentage of Chileans who say they feel "boredom," "indifference," or "antagonism" toward politics: 53

Percentage of the population of Nicaragua that is under 15: 47

Percentage of the population of Israel, Gaza, and the West Bank that is Jewish: 63

Portion of Poland's 200,000 heroin addicts who are under 21: $2/3$

Percentage of U.S. workers who were laid off between 1980 and 1986 and subsequently found work: 55.8

Percentage of them whose new jobs are lower-paying or part-time: 43.4

Portion of Yale's 1985 class that applied for jobs at First Boston: ⅓

ORNAMENTS

Percentage of Americans who invent a job or a college degree for their résumés: 10

Percentage of Harvard's class of 1986 who graduated with honors, yet had below-median grades: 21

Number of boxers who currently hold a world championship: 40

Wholesale price of an AK-47: $230

Number of stretch limousines sold in 1980: 2,000

In 1985: 6,000

Number of alligator farms in the United States: 23

Amount *The Triumph of Beauty*, a portrait of Imelda Marcos, brought at auction in 1986: $27,500

Plastic pink flamingos sold in the United States in 1985: 450,000

Number of women who serve on the board of the AFL-CIO: 2

PASTIMES

Length of the average American business lunch (in minutes): 67

Of the average French business lunch: 124

Percentage change in U.S. video-game sales since 1982: −75

In adult board game sales: +9

Frames bowled in U.S. ten-pin alleys in 1985: 7,839,859,000

Percentage of American parents who say they never read to their children: 40

Who never help them with their homework: 27

Percentage of all TV shows taped by Americans that are episodes of "All My Children": 4.4

Percentage of American adults who went on a diet in 1986: 25

Americans who say they have quit smoking: 37,000,000

Who say they haven't: 53,000,000

PLOYS

Number of states in which some part of the B-1 bomber is manufactured: 48

Number of states in which nuclear weapons are deployed: 27

Percentage of the Reagan administration's 1987 Star Wars budget that was allocated for "demonstration projects": 58

Number of times since 1979 that Britain has "refined" its method of counting the unemployed: 19

Number of those "refinements" that have resulted in a lower unemployment rate: 18

Rank of France, Italy, and England among destinations of congressional fact-finding trips: 1, 2, 3

Number of banks in the West that are owned by the Soviet Union: 6

Average percentage by which art that has been donated is overvalued for tax purposes: 600

Number of Americans currently frozen in the hope of one day coming back to life: 13

PRIORITIES

Amount spent by the University of Alabama on athletics in the 1985–86 academic year: $8,600,000

Amount spent by the University of Alabama on its physics department: $1,148,000

Percentage of the $2.1 billion federal antidrug budget that goes to law enforcement: 69

That goes to educational programs: 1

Amount that South Africa spends to educate the average white student each year (in rand): 1,385

The average "coloured" student: 872

The average black student: 192

Percentage of college freshmen who say that "being well-off financially" is important: 68.9

Who say that "developing a philosophy of life" is important: 46.7

Rank of Mass, bingo, and religious education among the most popular activities at U.S. Catholic churches: 1, 2, 3

Percentage of Americans who say that good sex is "very important" to a marriage: 75

Percentage of West Germans who say this: 52

Percentage of American married couples who say they argue about sex or adultery: 25

Who say they argue about money: 78

Percentage of Americans who say they would rather have a tooth pulled than take a car in for repairs: 20

Percentage of capital spending by U.S. companies that went for pollution controls in 1976: 5.6

In 1985: 2.7

Amount the military spent recruiting and training the 1,800 homosexuals it discharged in 1985: $22,138,200

Amount the Reagan administration budgeted for military bands in 1987: $154,200,000

Amount it budgeted for the National Endowment for the Arts: $144,900,000

PROCEDURES

Rank of sterilization among methods of birth control used in the United States: 1

Percentage of abortions in the United States that are performed on Catholic women: 29

Abortions per 1,000 live births in New York City: 852

Percentage of Seattleites who have had training in cardiopulmonary resuscitation: 40

Portion of the world's nations that have practiced torture since 1980: 1/3

Number of health professionals in Chile who specialize in treating the victims of torture: 50

Percentage of deaths in 1965 in which autopsies were performed: 41

Today: 14

Estimated percentage of boys born in the United States in 1985 who were circumcised: 70

Percentage of boys born in Britain who were: 0.4

Percentage of French women who say they've had sex in a movie theater: 2

Cost of having a car blessed at the Daishi Buddhist temple in Kawasaki, Japan: $10.77

Percentage of the U.S. potato crop that is french-fried: 22

QUOTIDIA

Amount of pizza consumed each day in the United States (in acres): 75

Percentage of Americans who eat at McDonald's each day: 7

Percentage of Americans who eat their evening meal between 5:00 P.M. and 8:00 P.M.: 87

Percentage increase since 1977 in the number of Americans who skip breakfast: 33

Percentage of Americans who say that Monday is their favorite day of the week: 3

Who say that Tuesday is: 1

Percentage of Americans who say they are at their best in the morning: 56

After midnight: 2

Number of different songs broadcast by Muzak each day: 480

Number of Americans who quit their jobs each workday: 60,000

Number of Americans who are fired each workday: 12,000

Rank of watching television among activities people look forward to during the day: 1

Number of Americans who drown in the bathtub each day: 1

REALPOLITIK

Number of countries that have switched sides in the Cold War: 28

Number of countries that have sold arms to both sides in the Iran-Iraq war: 8

Percentage increase since 1980 in political contributions by the top 20 defense contractors: 100

Strategic minerals supplied by the Soviet Union to the United States: 2

Vice versa: 1

Percentage increase in Angola's oil exports to the United States since 1982: 100

Percentage increase in trade between China and the Soviet Union in the first half of 1986: 58

American firms doing business in El Salvador: 51

In Nicaragua: 48

Number of South Africans who changed their citizenship in order to compete in the 1984 Olympics: 6

Number of delegates to the 1980 Democratic convention not chosen in a primary or caucus: 0

Number of such delegates to the 1984 convention: 873

Percentage of Chicago public school teachers who send their children to private or parochial schools: 38

Percentage of all life forms known to have existed that exist today: 0.01

RECEIVABLES

Amount the IRS claims John Walker owes in back taxes on income he earned from spying: $193,000

Amount the IRS claims G. Gordon Liddy owes in back taxes on Watergate slush funds that he spent: $20,449

Percentage of federal criminal fines levied in the past 16 years that remain unpaid: 45

Percentage of mothers who do not receive the court-ordered child support to which they are entitled: 24

REVOLUTION (Post-Industrial)

Number of Americans who have someone else's heart: 300

Number of Americans who were conceived in a test tube: 700

Number of Americans conceived by artificial insemination: 450,000

Number of years it takes for the information stored in all the world's libraries and computers to double: 8

Watts required to operate an IBM personal computer: 93

Watts of power used by the human brain when it is engaged in deep thought: 14

Percentage of Forbes 500 chief executive officers in 1979 who had a technical background: 12.7

In 1985: 18.2

Value of insurance claims filed for satellite launch failures in 1985: $336,500,000

Percentage of American households whose TV sets have remote control: 51.3

Percentage of Americans who think science and technology may destroy the human race: 74

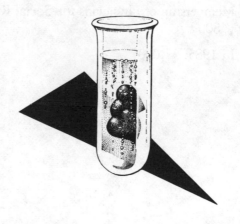

REVOLUTION (Reagan)

Percentage of labor negotiations since 1983 that have resulted in union "givebacks": 20

Percentage of all federal judges appointed during Reagan's first term who graduated from Ivy League schools: 10

Percentage change in the number of federal employees since 1981: +5

Percentage increase in capital spending by business during the first Reagan administration: 23

During the Carter administration: 32

Percentage of capital spending by U.S. companies that went for worker health and safety items in 1978: 2.9

In 1985: 1.8

Percentage of U.S. foreign aid in 1980 that consisted of military assistance: 25

In 1986: 40

Percentage change since 1981 in the amount the Pentagon spends on classified projects: +300

Percentage of new government R&D spending that went to Star Wars in 1986: 22

Membership of Physicians for Social Responsibility in 1980: 800

In 1985: 32,000

REVOLUTION (Sexual)

Percentage of American women who think they would do "better than average" in a fistfight: 27

Percentage who thought this in 1977: 19

Number of U.S. firms that offered child-care benefits in 1978: 115

In 1986: 3,000

Percentage of fathers who win child custody cases they contest: 70

Percentage increase, since 1980, in the number of lawyers who specialize in divorce: 100

Percentage of men who say they are happier since their divorce or separation: 58

Percentage of women who say this: 85

Percentage of Americans buying stocks for the first time who are women: 57

Percentage of American women who said they liked sports cars in 1976: 39

Who say that today: 56

Percentage of the 7,791,000 new jobs created since 1979 that were filled by women: 88

Percentage of new members of the AFL-CIO in 1986 who are women: 55

Percentage increase in the number of women in U.S. prisons since 1974: 285

Percentage of women executives who say they prefer a male boss: 29

Who say they prefer a female boss: 4

Ratio of male to female ulcer patients in the United States in 1966: 20 to 1

Today: 2 to 1

RISKS

Years a Zimbabwean can be imprisoned for ridiculing President Canaan Banana: 5

Number of countries in which a citizen can be penalized for not voting: 19

Maximum fine for refusing to register for the draft in the United States: $250,000

Combined prison sentence for everyone convicted of insider trading since 1934 (in years): 14

Percentage of all venture capital funds that were invested in leveraged buyouts in 1983: 14

In 1985: 21

Percentage of all corporate-bond debt issued in 1978 that was rated "A" or better: 81

Percentage issued in 1985 that was: 64

Chances that a taxpayer's returns will be audited: 1 in 66

Chances that a black American man will be murdered: 1 in 21

Percentage of Americans who commit murder and never appear in a courtroom: 24

Percentage of college men who say they might commit rape if there was no chance of being caught: 35

Percentage of married women in the United States who say they have been raped by their husbands: 14

Number of states in which marital rape is not a crime: 29

Deaths and disabling injuries per 1,000 miners in 1985: 30

Per 1,000 farmers: 60

Number of Americans struck by lightning each year: 350

Percentage of homeowners in California who have earthquake insurance: 10

Chances that one of the 100 operating U.S. nuclear reactors will melt down in the next 20 years: 45 in 100

Percentage of Iowans whose drinking water contains traces of one or more pesticides: 27

Percentage of nursing mothers in the United States whose milk contains traces of PCBs: 87

Average number of new recipes tried in American households every month: 1.6

RITES (of Passage)

Average age at which an American first gets a watch: 6½

Average age at which American girls began to menstruate in 1900: 14.3

Today: 12.9

Average age at which an inmate in federal prison first fired a gun: 13.2

First had sex: 13.7

Percentage of adults who say they were first told the facts of life by their mothers: 21

By their fathers: 5

Percentage of teenagers who lost their virginity in a car: 12

In their own or their partner's home: 54

Chances that a working American has worked at a McDonald's: 1 in 15

Percentage of American marriages that occur in June: 12

Number of weddings performed each day in 1985 at Las Vegas's Little Church of the West: 163

SECOND THOUGHTS

Percentage of American teachers who say that if they could start over, they would not teach: 24

Percentage who said that in 1965: 7.1

Days spent on strike by British workers in 1979: 29,474,000

In 1985: 6,372,000

Percentage of American adults over 50 who say their current occupation is different from what they planned when young: 45

Percentage of acknowledged male homosexuals who are fathers: 25

Percentage of defectors who eventually return to their homelands: 50

SENTIMENTS

Valentine's Day cards purchased by Americans in 1986: 950,000,000

Cut roses (in dozens): 5,400,000

Percentage of Americans who say they have been "moved to tears" by a greeting card: 29

Percentage of married men who say they would marry the same woman if they had it to do all over again: 80

Percentage of women who say they would marry the same man: 50

Percentage of Italian women who say they are more romantic than their husbands: 62

Percentage of Americans who say they approve of the use of monkeys in medical experiments: 69

Percentage of teenagers who say they favor a one-year national youth service program for men: 62

Percentage of Greeks who say they are willing to fight for their country: 76

Percentage of West Germans who say this: 33

Percentage of Iowans who say that front-porch swings "should be brought back": 57

Rank of blue among Americans' favorite colors: 1

Percentage of Americans who say that spring fever makes them sad: 4

STANDARDS AND PRACTICES

Percentage of Americans who say they support the 55-mile-per-hour speed limit: 70

Percentage of drivers on interstate highways who exceed the 55-mile-per-hour speed limit: 77

Number of pedestrians issued summonses for jaywalking in New York City in 1985: 1,800

In Los Angeles: 50,000

Rank of the Soviet Union, South Africa, and the United States in per capita prison population: 1, 2, 3

Percentage of U.S. Supreme Court cases in which civil liberties claims were made and upheld in 1963: 86

In 1985: 44

Percentage of the sexual acts depicted or referred to on prime-time TV that are between married partners: 6

Estimated percentage of all U.S. defense contracts that are awarded through thoroughly competitive bidding: 5

Number of times Senate rules permit a senator to use his own name on each page of his newsletter: 8

Average number of maggots the U.S. Food and Drug Administration permits per 100 grams of canned mushrooms: 20

Percentage of American parents who say they spank their children: 83

Percentage of those who say they consider spanking seldom, if ever, effective: 40

SUBTRACTIONS

Number of American shoe factories that close each week: 1

Number of coffin manufacturers in the United States today: 400

Fifteen years ago: 600

Percentage change in Britain's manufacturing output since 1979: −6

Percentage by which China plans to reduce the size of its army by 1988: 25

Portion of El Salvador controlled by guerrillas in 1980: ¼

Portion controlled by guerrillas today: ⅛

Percentage of practicing physicians who belonged to the American Medical Association in 1962: 74

Today: 45

Percentage decrease since 1970 in the number of deaths due to heart disease: 28

In the number of deaths due to strokes: 49

Estimated percentage of U.S. crops lost to insects each year: 13

Percentage of Americans between the ages of 15 and 19 who say they have shoplifted: 43

SUPERSTITIONS

Percentage of Americans who believed in 1973 that communism is the worst form of government: 44

Percentage who believe that today: 59

Percentage of Americans who say that some numbers are especially lucky for some people: 40

Astronomers in the United States: 3,650

Astrologers: 15,000

Percentage decrease in the number of science books published in the United States since 1972: 50

Percentage of health articles in *Cosmopolitan* rated inaccurate by the American Council on Science and Health: 53

Of articles in *Prevention:* 69

Percentage of Americans' disposable income that is spent on insurance premiums: 11

Percentage of Americans who believe their presence at a sports event influences its outcome: 25

Percentage of Icelanders who believe in elves: 5

SUSPICIONS

Percentage of Americans who believe files are being kept on them for unknown reasons: 67

Percentage who believed this in 1974: 44

Percentage increase in wiretaps authorized by federal judges since 1980: 200

Percentage change, in 1985, in the number of federal employees with security clearances: − 21

Number of Americans who were tested by urinalysis for drug use in 1985: 4,500,000

Portion of Fortune 1000 companies that employed undercover security agents in 1974: 1/10

In 1985: 1/2

Number of documents classified top secret by the U.S. government since 1979: 3,530,177

Portion of the U.S. landmass off-limits to Soviet officials: 1/5

Percentage of Americans who say that France is not a reliable ally: 54

Percentage of Australian business executives who say the Japanese are untrustworthy and unethical: 89

Percentage of Americans who say that U.S. space shots have caused changes in the weather: 41

Percentage of Americans who think the afterlife will be boring: 5

TALK

Number of people who try unsuccessfully to get President Reagan on the telephone each year: 175,000

Number of "telephone-related" injuries in 1985: 11,000

Amount that Robin Weir, Nancy Reagan's hairdresser, charges for a haircut: $150

Amount he charges for a speech: $1,000

Number of schools that invited Lee Iacocca to speak at their graduation ceremonies in 1986: 150

Number that invited Mario Cuomo: 160

Percentage of Congressmen who say that virtuous living is the path to salvation: 39

Number of times the CIA briefed its congressional oversight committees in 1985: 500

Pentagon phone bill in 1986: $84,800,000

Amount the United States spent in 1985 on radio broadcasts to Eastern Europe and the Soviet Union: $146,559,000

Estimated amount the Soviet Union spent trying to jam those broadcasts: $300,000,000

Percentage of Americans who say they believe "most" or "all" of what Dan Rather says: 81

Number of U.S. residents five years of age or older who do not speak English: 1,218,000

Rank of *indifferent, apathy,* and *obscure* among the vocabulary words appearing most frequently on the SAT: 1, 2, 3

Percentage of Americans who say they have never heard the word *yuppie:* 39

TASKS

Pieces of paper processed by American businesses in 1986: 1,680,000,000,000

Number of unnecessary photocopies that will be made at businesses in 1985: 130,000,000

Number of rescues made by lifeguards on Southern California beaches in 1985: 33,278

Number of countries whose armed forces are combating a revolutionary or separatist insurgency: 30

Number of federal commissions appointed to study the Pentagon since 1949: 35

Number of aircraft-maintenance forms filled out each day in the navy: 66,000

Number of times Rod McKuen says he rewrote his book *The Sound of Solitude:* 34

Cans of soda that Pepsi must sell to recoup the cost of its Michael Jackson advertising campaign: 192,307,692

Number of faces the average person learns and remembers throughout his lifetime: 10,000

Minutes of each workday that the average American spends earning money to pay taxes: 159

Amount Americans spend to have their federal tax returns prepared each year: $11,700,000,000

Decimal places to which the value of *pi* has been calculated: 134,217,700

TRANSIENTS

Number of heads of government in the United States since 1964: 5

In the Soviet Union: 4

In Switzerland: 17

Number of jobs filled each day by temporary workers in 1980: 416,000

In 1986: 700,000

Number of jobs the average worker has held by age 40: 8

Number of homes the average person lives in over a lifetime: 30

Years the average homeless person lives on the street: 7

Percentage of American families that own three or more cars: 23

Percentage of Americans who live in mobile homes: 4.6

Number of cabooses in America: 10,255

WAYS AND MEANS

Percentage of all hostage deaths in airplane hijackings since 1968 that occurred during rescue attempts: 85

Number of prisoners on death row who have committed suicide, been murdered, or have died of natural causes since 1977: 39

Number who were executed: 68

Percentage of Americans who die in health-care institutions: 80

Deaths by gunshot in the movie *Scarface*: 41

By strangulation or hanging: 3

By chain saw: 1

Percentage of all playground injuries that occur on the monkey bars: 55

WINDFALLS

Price of an Exocet missile on the world market before the 1982 Falklands War: $280,000

Price today: $500,000

Total amount that NBC's four Thursday-night sitcoms are expected to earn in syndication: $1,000,000,000

Average amount wagered, per capita, in state lotteries in 1985: $92.61

Pairs of socks received as gifts by Vice-President George Bush: 48

WORRIES

Rank, among situations that make adults anxious, of being at a party with strangers: 1

Percentage of American teenagers who report that their schoolwork makes them anxious: 82

Who report that their love life does: 57

Percentage of teenage boys who say they worry about losing their hair: 29

Percentage of teenage girls who say this: 36

Percentage of American college students who spend more than half their waking hours worrying: 15

Percentage of American women who consider themselves pretty: 13

Percentage of American men who consider themselves handsome: 28

Percentage of American car owners who keep maps in their glove compartments: 50

Percentage of Fortune 500 executives who say they "lose sleep over the competition": 13.7

YIELDS

Jobs created by every billion dollars of U.S. government defense spending: 25,000

By every billion dollars of nondefense spending: 25,000

Rank of marijuana, corn, and soybeans, among all U.S. crops, in annual cash value: 1, 2, 3

Gross national home gardening product in 1985: $8,300,000,000

Percentage increase in world food production since 1974: 30

Pounds of redfish harvested from the Gulf of Mexico in 1982: 2,400,000

In 1985: 5,700,000

Garbage produced daily at the Oceanside Holiday Inn in Fort Lauderdale in March (in dumpsters): 78

During the rest of the year: 3

Average bank robbery take: $3,000

Average amount stolen by pickpockets, per incident: $218

By shoplifters: $72

Rank of Mississippi, among all states, in the number of professional football players produced per capita: 1

Average number of points scored in a National Football League game in 1985: 43

Total baseball at-bats in the major leagues in 1986: 143,106

Home runs: 3,813

ZEROS

Number of jobs added to the economy by the Fortune 500 since 1980: 0

Regularly scheduled prime-time variety shows on network TV: 0

Copies of *Duarte: My Story*, the autobiography of El Salvador's president, published in Spanish: 0

Number of weeks, since December 1981, that Danielle Steele has not had a book on a best-seller list: 0

Percentage of American car owners who keep gloves in their glove compartments: 0

SOURCES

What follows are the sources for all of the statistics in this volume. (The numbering corresponds to the order of statistics in each rubric.) In general, the source is the individual or institution with whom our researchers spoke to confirm the figure's accuracy. When a statistic has come to our attention by way of the media, we have made an effort to contact the person or group who originally calculated the figure, conducted the survey, or counted the items in question. In some cases, the person most knowledgeable about a particular number is an author, and here we list the person's name and publication. Where multiple sources are joined by "and," this indicates that two or more people or institutions together developed a single statistic; a slash indicates that we combined information from more than one source to produce the statistic. The citation "*Harper's* research" indicates that we either used information from several other sources to produce a new statistic, or performed the primary research ourselves. In all cases, statistics are the latest available as of fall 1986.

PA

ADDITIONS
1. American Society of Plastic and Reconstructive Surgeons (Chicago)
2. Internal Revenue Service
3. Community Youth Gang Services Project (Los Angeles)
4. U.S. Department of Justice
5. American Correctional Association (College Park, Md.)
6., 7. National Spa and Pool Institute (Alexandria, Va.)
8. James Lovelock and Michael Allaby, *The Greening of Mars* (New York: Marek/St. Martins Press, 1984)

91

9., 10. *Public Citizen* (Common Cause, Washington, D.C.)
11., 12. National Hospice Association (Arlington, Va.)
13. Polish Consulate (New York)
14. Church of Jesus Christ of Latter-Day Saints (Salt Lake City)
15. Federal Reserve Bank of Boston
16. Yale University (New Haven, Conn.)
17. *The Wall Street Journal*
18. Dataquest (San Jose, Calif.)

ALARMS

1., 2. Risks International (Alexandria, Va.)
3., 4. Center for Defense Information (Washington, D.C.)
5., 6. Nuclear Control Institute (Washington, D.C.)
7., 8. U.S. Office of Technology Assessment
9., 10. *The Futurist* (Washington, D.C.)
11., 12. National Center for Health Statistics (Hyattsville, Md.)
13. New York City Department of Health
14. "The Changing Face of Poverty," by Dr. Emanuel Tobier of New
York University, for the Community Service Society of New
York
15. Centers for Disease Control (Atlanta)
16. Federal Deposit Insurance Corporation (Washington, D.C.)
17. *Sprint* (Scholastic, Inc., New York)
18. Dr. Ernest Hartmann, Tufts University Medical School (Medford,
Mass.)

AMBITIONS

1. Media General (Richmond, Va.) and Associated Press (New York)
Poll
2. Roper Organization (New York)
3. Erdos & Morgan (New York)
4., 5. U.S. Bureau of the Census
6. Dale Carnegie and Associates (Garden City, N.Y.)
7. Universal Esperanto Association (New York)
8. Simplified Spelling Society (Southampton, England)

ANACHRONISMS

1. U.S. State Department
2. World Health Organization (Washington, D.C.)
3. Centers for Disease Control (Atlanta)
4. Ivor Spencer School for British Butlers and Administrators (London)
5. American Council of Nanny Schools (Midland, Mich.)
6. *The Spectator* (London)
7. Miss America Pageant (Atlantic City)
8. Jostens (Minneapolis), diploma printers
9. *American Demographics* (Ithaca, N.Y.)
10. Jack Colhoun (Washington, D.C.), former editor of *AMEX-Canada*
11. Professor Benjamin Zablocki, Department of Sociology, Rutgers University (New Brunswick, N.J.)
12. International Maritime Bureau (London)
13. International Flat Earth Research Society (Lancaster, Calif.)

ANOMALIES

1. *Electronic Media* (Chicago)
2. *The World Almanac and Book of Facts 1986* (New York: Newspaper Enterprise Association)
3. Brule Ville Associés (Paris)
4. Abraham Lincoln Association (Springfield, Ill.)
5. Calvin Coolidge Memorial Foundation (Plymouth, Vt.)
6., 7. Irving Wallace, et al., *The Book of Lists #2* (New York: William Morrow, 1980)
8., 9. SAMI (New York)
10., 11. Audit Bureau of Circulation (Schaumburg, Ill.)
12., 13. International Association of Ice Cream Manufacturers (Washington, D.C.)
14. American Cancer Society (New York)
15., 16. International Association for Bear Research and Management (Calgary, Alberta)

APPEARANCES

1., 2. Gallup Organization (Princeton, N.J.)
3. Cadwell Davis Partners (New York)
4. John Deere & Company (Moline, Ill.)

5. Steve's Detailing (New York)
6. Procter & Gamble (Cincinnati)
7. *People* (New York)
8. Jack Nicholson (Los Angeles)
9. Sammy Davis, Jr. (Beverly Hills, Calif.)
10., 11. National Aeronautics and Space Administration

APPETITES

1. U.S. Department of Agriculture
2. U.S. Food and Drug Administration
3. Coca-Cola U.S.A. (Atlanta)
4. Gallup Organization (Princeton, N.J.)
5., 6. *Money* (New York)
7. J. D. Power and Associates (Westlake Village, Calif.)
8. Ruth Leger Sivard, *World Military and Social Expenditures, 1986* (Washington, D.C.: World Priorities)
9. Arms Control and Disarmament Agency (Washington, D.C.)
10., 11. Paul Murphy, "The Military Tax Bite, 1986" (Washington, D.C.: Military Spending Research Services)
12. *The Wall Street Journal*
13., 14. U.S. Department of Agriculture
15., 16. International Association of Ice Cream Manufacturers (Washington, D.C.)
17. Fauchon (Paris)
18. *The New York Times*
19., 20. New York City Department of Health

BARGAINS

1. U.S. Department of Defense
2. Washington Analysis Corporation (Washington, D.C.)
3. Occupational Safety and Health Administration
4. Internal Revenue Service
5. Citizens for Tax Justice (Washington, D.C.)
6., 7. Professor James Clayton, provost, University of Utah (Salt Lake City)
8., 9. National Gardening Association (Burlington, Vt.)
10. North Country Corporation (Cambridge, Mass.)
11. National Ski Areas Association (Springfield, Mass.)

12., 13. Joseph Berman Realty (Brooklyn, N.Y.)
14. Solair (Southbridge, Mass.)

BLACK AND WHITE

1. Hastings Center (Hastings-on-Hudson, N.Y.)
2. NAACP Legal Defense and Education Fund (New York)
3. U.S. Bureau of the Census
4., 5. National Opinion Research Center (Chicago)
6. Manning Marable, *Black American Politics* (New York: Schocken Books, 1985)
7. Joint Center for Political Studies (Washington, D.C.)
8. Professor John C. Phillips, Department of Sociology, University of the Pacific (Stockton, Calif.)
9., 10. Media General (Richmond) and Associated Press (New York) Poll
11., 12. National Opinion Research Center (Chicago)

CHIMERA

1. Audits and Surveys (San Francisco)
2. U.S. Department of Justice
3. *Denver Post*
4. Risks International
5., 6. Center for Defense Information (Washington, D.C.)
7. National Climatic Data Center (Asheville, N.C.)
8. Metropolitan Museum of Art (New York)
9. U.S. Customs Service
10. *Journalism Quarterly* (University of South Carolina at Columbia)
11. Penelope Leach, *The Child Care Encyclopedia* (New York: Alfred A. Knopf, 1984)
12. National Institute of Mental Health (Bethesda, Md.)
13. New York City Police Department

COMEBACKS

1., 2. New Jersey Department of Environmental Protection (Trenton)
3., 4. National Wildlife Federation (Washington, D.C.)
5. Viacom Productions (Los Angeles)
6. American Council on Education (Washington, D.C.)
7. Central Intelligence Agency

8. U.S. Peace Corps
9. U.S. Drug Enforcement Agency

COMFORTS

1. A. C. Nielsen (New York)
2. The HUMOR Project (Sagamore Institute, Saratoga Springs, N.Y.)
3. Alcohol Research Information Service (Lansing, Mich.)
4. Counter Spy Shop (Washington, D.C.)
5. Jerry Falwell (Lynchburg, Va.)
6., 7. Hewitt Associates (Lincolnshire, Ill.)
8. Dr. Stephen Holzman (Nassau-Suffolk Veterinary Hospital, Farmingdale, N.Y.)
9. International Pet Cemetery Association (South Bend, Ind.)
10. Lobel Brothers Prime Meats (New York)
11. *Snack Food* (Duluth, Minn.)
12. "Attorney General's Commission on Pornography Report" (U.S. Government Printing Office, 1986)
13. Romantic Times, Inc. (Brooklyn)
14. A. C. Nielsen (New York)
15. *P.M. Magazine* (San Francisco)
16., 17. Roper Organization (New York)
18., 19. Gallup Organization (Princeton, N.J.)

CONDITIONS

1. United Nations High Commissioner on Refugees (New York)
2. Raymond D. Gastil, *Freedom in the World, 1985–1986* (New York: Greenwood Press, 1985)
3. U.S. Bureau of the Census
4. U.S. Veterans Administration
5., 6. American Psychiatric Association (Washington, D.C.)
7. Search Institute (Minneapolis)
8. National Opinion Research Center (Chicago)

CONFIRMATIONS

1. *Journal of the American Medical Association* (Chicago)
2. *Detroit Free Press*
3. American Sports Data (Hartsdale, N.Y.)
4., 5. R. H. Bruskin (New Brunswick, N.J.)

6. Heidrick & Struggles (New York)
7., 8. *U.S. News and World Report* (Washington, D.C.)
9. John Sineno, author of *The Firefighter's Cookbook* (New York: Vintage Books, 1986)
10. *The Times* (London)
11. National Pasta Association (Arlington, Va.)
12. U.S. Bureau of the Census
13. Massachusetts Institute of Technology (Cambridge)
14. U.S. Table Tennis Association (Colorado Springs)
15., 16. *One Medicine: A Tribute to Kurt Benirschke*, eds. O. A. Ryder and M. L. Byrd (Berlin: Springer-Verlag, 1984)
17. Roper Organization (New York)

CONSEQUENCES

1. Cognos Associates (Los Altos, Calif.)
2., 3. Council on Economic Priorities (New York)
4. Peter J. Brancazio, *Sport Science* (New York: Simon & Schuster, 1984)
5. U.S. Bureau of Justice Statistics
6., 7. Lenore J. Weitzman, *The Divorce Revolution: The Unexpected Social and Economic Consequences for Women and Children in America* (New York: Free Press/Macmillan, 1985)
8., 9. Korn/Ferry International (New York)
10. Price Waterhouse (Houston)
11. National Governors' Association and the National Association of State Budget Officers (Washington, D.C.)
12., 13. *Dissent* (New York)
14. Atlantic City Police Department

CONVERSIONS

1. South African Institute of Race Relations (Johannesburg)
2., 3. Professor John Petrocik, Department of Political Science, University of California (Los Angeles)
4. North American Congress on Latin America (New York)
5. National Council for U.S.-China Trade (Washington, D.C.)
6. Beijing International Golf Club
7. British Consulate (New York)
8., 9. Alan Sager, "The Reconfiguration of Urban Hospital Care," in *Cities and Sickness* (Beverly Hills: Sage Publications, 1983)

10. National Institute of Corrections (U.S. Department of Justice)
11. National Council on Crime and Delinquency (Madison, Wis.)
12., 13. Goldman Sachs Research (New York)
14., 15. American Airlines (Forth Worth, Texas)

CROSSOVERS

1. Dr. Stanley H. Biber (Trinidad, Colo.)
2., 3. *Working Woman* (New York)
4. Kellogg Company (Battle Creek, Mich.)
5. Des Moines Register and Tribune Company
6. Recording Industry Association of America (New York)
7. U.S. Government Accounting Office, "D.O.D. Revolving Door: Relationships Between Work at D.O.D. and Post-D.O.D. Employment" (U.S. Government Printing Office, 1986)
8. New York City Police Department
9., 10. Media General (Richmond) and Associated Press (New York) Poll
11. 1984 National Survey of American Jews (American Jewish Committee, New York)

CUSTOMS

1., 2. *Harper's* research
3., 4. Des Moines Register and Tribune Company
5. California Department of Public Works Recycling Program (Berkeley)
6. U.S. Bureau of Labor Statistics
7. Mark Greenfield, W. Averell Harriman Institute for Advanced Study of the Soviet Union, Columbia University (New York)
8. U.S. Bureau of Labor Statistics
9. New York City Police Department
10. Los Angeles County Sheriff's Department
11. NAACP Legal Defense and Educational Fund (New York City)
12. *The Atlantic* (Boston)
13., 14. Cremation Association of North America (Chicago)
15., 16. Alan Guttmacher Institute (New York City)
17., 18. National Committee for Adoption (Washington, D.C.)
19. Market Compilation and Research Bureau (North Hollywood, Calif.)
20. U.S. Bureau of the Census
21., 22. MRCA Information Services (Stamford, Conn.)
23. Runzheimer International (Rochester, Wis.)

DAYDREAMS

1., 2. Roper Organization (New York)
3. David Barlow, director, Sexuality Research Program, State University of New York (Albany)
4. *Crain's New York Business*
5. American Motors Company (Detroit)
6. Pan Am (New York)
7. *Chicago Sun-Times*
8., 9. *Harper's* research
10. North American Congress on Latin America (New York)
11. New Jersey Department of Corrections (Trenton)
12. National Association of Professional Baseball Leagues (St. Petersburg)
13., 14. *Sports Illustrated* Sports Poll 1986 (New York)
15., 16. Professors Lorraine Prinsky, Department of Sociology; and Jill Rosenbaum, Department of Criminology, California State University (Fullerton)

DELIVERIES

1., 2. *American Baby* (New York)
3. Henny Youngman (New York)
4., 5. U.S. Department of Energy
6. Port Authority of New York and New Jersey
7. Worldport (Los Angeles)
8. National Organization for the Reform of Marijuana Laws (Washington, D.C.)
9. National Restaurant Association (Washington, D.C.)
10. U.S. Postal Service
11. *The New York Times*

DISAPPEARANCES

1. United Nations Food and Agricultural Organization (New York)
2. U.S. Postal Service
3. U.S. General Services Administration
4. U.S. State Department
5. *The New York Times*
6., 7. U.S. Department of Defense
8. Latin American Federation of Families of Disappeared Prisoners (Caracas, Venezuela)

9., 10. *Harper's* research
11., 12. League of American Theaters and Producers
13. Radio Information Center (New York)
14. Trooper Guy Kimball (Bedford, N.H.)
15. National Institute of Mental Health (Bethesda, Md.)
16. Chicago Public Library

DISPARITIES

1. *USA Today*
2. Miami Police Department
3., 4. *Time* (New York)
5. U.S. Agency for International Development
6. U.S. Department of Commerce
7. Robert W. Crandall, Brookings Institution (Washington, D.C.)
8. United Auto Workers (Detroit)
9. Stagehands Local 1 (New York)
10., 11. U.S. Bureau of Labor Statistics
12., 13. Sylvania A. Hewlett, *A Lesser Life: The Myth of Women's Liberation in America* (New York: William Morrow, 1986)
14. Robert Meyers, former director of Social Security Administration (Washington, D.C.)
15. Office of Family Assistance (U.S. Department of Health and Human Services)
16., 17. National League of Cities (Washington, D.C.)
18., 19. U.S. Federal Aviation Administration
20., 21. National Criminal Justice Reference Service (Rockville, Md.)

DISPLAYS

1., 2. Professor William Frey, Department of Psychology, University of Minnesota (St. Paul)
3. Personalized Plate Section, Office of the Secretary of State of Illinois (Springfield)
4. Environmental License Plate Unit, California State Department of Motor Vehicles (Sacramento)
5. BMW North America (Montvale, N.J.)
6. Rolls-Royce Motor Cars (Crewe, England)
7. Cunard Line (New York)
8. Dettra Flag Company (Oaks, Pa.)

9. Federal Bureau of Investigation
10. "Latenight with David Letterman" (New York)
11. *Harper's* research
12. The New York Mets (Flushing, N.Y.)
13., 14. Goddard Space Flight Center (Greenbelt, Md.)
15. ISL Marketing A.G. (New York)
16. Steger International Polar Expedition (Ely, Minn.)
17. "21" Club (New York)

DIVERSIONS

1. U.S. Bureau of the Census
2. *Variety* (New York)
3. *1985 UNESCO Statistical Yearbook*
4. Borden, Inc. (Columbus, Ohio)
5., 6. Food Marketing Institute (Washington, D.C.)
7., 8. Tom Biracree, *How You Rate: Men* (New York: Dell Publishing, 1984)

ENTHUSIASMS

1. Florida Department of Corrections (Tallahassee)
2., 3. Gallup Organization (Princeton, N.J.)
4. Roper Organization (New York)
5. National Center for Health Statistics (Hyattsville, Md.)
6. ABC News (New York) and *Washington Post* Poll
7. American Accordionists Association (New York)
8. WORD (Waco, Tex.)
9. Des Moines Register & Tribune Company
10. Uncle Milton Industries, Inc. (Culver City, Calif.)
11. Baseball Hall of Fame (Cooperstown, N.Y.)
12. Pat Paulsen (Cloverdale, Calif.)

EPHEMERA

1. Shaw Creations (New York)
2. American Museum of Natural History (New York)
3. Rawlings Sporting Goods Company (St. Louis)
4. *Advertising Age* (New York)
5. Point of Purchase Advertising Institute (Fort Lee, N.J.)

6., 7. Marketing Evaluations (Port Washington, N.Y.)
8. Al Goldstein, editor, *Screw* (New York)
9., 10. Society for the Scientific Study of Sex (Philadelphia)

EQUIVALENCES

1. Fairfield Group (Stamford, Conn.)
2. U.S. Department of Education
3. Center for Public Resources (New York)
4. Nell Eurich, "Corporate Classrooms" (Princeton, N.J.: Carnegie Foundation for the Advancement of Teaching, 1985)
5., 6. James S. Henry, "The Mexican Debt Crisis" (unpublished paper)
7. Dickstein, Shapiro & Morin (Washington, D.C.)
8. Legal Services Corporation (Washington, D.C.)
9., 10. Congressional Joint Committee on Taxation
11. "Wheel of Fortune" (Burbank, Calif.)
12. National Basketball Players Association
13. *1986 Statistical Abstract of the United States* (U.S. Government Printing Office)
14. U.S. Bureau of Justice Statistics

EXITS AND ENTRANCES

1. U.S. Highway Traffic Safety Administration
2. U.S. Bureau of the Census
3. Norbert Gleisher, M.D. (Mount Sinai Hospital, Chicago), "Caesarian Section Rates in the U.S.," in *Journal of the American Medical Association* (Chicago)
4. National Center for Health Statistics (Hyattsville, Md.)
5. People for the Ethical Treatment of Animals (Washington, D.C.)
6. Tom Parker, *In One Day* (Boston: Houghton Mifflin, 1984)
7. Roper Organization (New York)
8. Population Reference Bureau (Washington, D.C.)
9. U.S. Department of Labor
10., 11. U.S. Department of Commerce
12. *New Product Development Newsletter* (New York)
13., 14. U.S. Bureau of Labor Statistics
15. U.S. Department of Defense
16. U.S. State Department/*Harper's* research

17. National Center for Health Statistics (Hyattsville, Md.)
18. New York City Police Department/*Harper's* research

EXPOSURES

1., 2. R. H. Bruskin (New Brunswick, N.J.)
3., 4. Federal Bureau of Investigation
5. American Bar Association (Washington, D.C.)
6., 7. *People* (New York)
8. Roper Organization (New York)
9. Eastman Kodak (Rochester, N.Y.)
10., 11. Roper Organization
12. *Harper's* research
13. Warner-Lambert Company (Morris Plains, N.J.)
14. Centers for Disease Control (Atlanta)

FAÇADES

1. Morley Safer (CBS News, New York)
2., 3. *Harper's* research
4. *Africa News* (Durham, N.C.)
5., 6. U.S. Air Force
7. U.S. Department of Defense
8., 9. *Advertising Age* (New York)
10. U.S. Savings and Loan Insurance Corporation
11. U.S. House Subcommittee on Health and Long-term Care
12. *Consumers Digest* (Chicago)
13. Little Jack Horner Joke and Magic Shop (Boston)

FADS

1. Campbell Communications, Inc. (Bethesda, Md.)
2. National Organization for the Reform of Marijuana Laws (Washington, D.C.)/*Harper's* research
3. Bruce Sanford, attorney, Baker & Hostetler (Washington, D.C.)
4. Hasbro, Inc. (Pawtucket, R.I.)
5., 6. Project of the Vietnam Generation (Smithsonian Institution)
7., 8. National Organization for Changing Men (Harriman, Tenn.)
9. Institutes for the Achievement of Human Potential (Philadelphia)

10. Camp Doll-Me (Machias, Me.)
11., 12. Los Angeles Dodgers
13. Smart, Inc. (Wilton, Conn.)
14. J. D. Power and Associates (Westlake Village, Calif.)
15., 16. National Association of Television Programming Executives (New York)
17., 18. Radio Information Center (New York)
19. *Billboard* (New York)

FREAKS AND WONDERS

1. *Variety* (New York)
2. *Publishers Weekly* (New York)
3. William H. Whyte (New York)
4. Holstein Association (Brattleboro, Vt.)
5. World Pumpkin Federation (Collins, N.Y.)
6. International Flying Chicken Association (Rio Grande, Ohio)

FRUITS AND VEGETABLES

1., 2. "National Food Review" (U.S. Department of Agriculture)
3., 4. Produce Marketing Association (Newark, Del.)
5. U.S. Bureau of Labor Statistics
6., 7. National Gardening Association (Burlington, Vt.)
8., 9. U.S. Department of Agriculture
10. Gallup Poll Ltd. (London)
11. Janet K. Rothrock, "Summary of the Evidence in Findings and Conclusions Concerning the Adverse Health Effects of Snuff" (Boston: Massachusetts Department of Health, 1985)
12. Ada County Elections Office (Boise, Idaho)

GRAND TOTALS

1. Donald Knowler, *The Falconer of Central Park* (New York: Bantam Books, 1986)
2. U.S. Geological Survey/*Harper's* research
3. Can Manufacturers Institute (Washington, D.C.)
4., 5. *Harper's* research
6. Short Snout Society (Greenville, S.C.)
7. Piggie Park Restaurant (Columbia, S.C.)

8. David Hooper and Kenneth Whyld, *Oxford Companion to Chess* (New York: Oxford University Press, 1984)
9. King Research (Rockville, Md.)
10. Montague Ullman and Nan Zimmerman, *Working with Dreams* (Los Angeles: Jeremy P. Tarcher Books, 1985)
11. Coca-Cola U.S.A. (Atlanta)
12. Charles Turner and Elizabeth Martin, *Surveying Subjective Phenomena*, Volume 1 (New York: Russell Sage Foundation, 1985)
13. *National Law Journal* (New York)
14. U.S. Department of the Treasury
15. *Forbes* (New York)
16. Professor Joseph Silk, Department of Astronomy, University of California (Berkeley)

GUNS AND BUTTER

1. U.S. Consumer Price Index/U.S. Department of Defense

HEGEMONY (American)

1. World Vision Enterprises (New York)
2. *U.S. News and World Report* (Washington, D.C.)
3. Bantam Books (New York)
4. *The New York Times*
5. *Newsweek* (New York)
6. Pencil Makers Association (Moorestown, N.J.)
7. U.S. Department of Commerce
8. *Electronic Media* (Chicago)
9., 10. Mike Williams, *The Wall Street Journal*
11., 12. W. Averell Harriman Institute for Advanced Study of the Soviet Union, Columbia University (New York)
13. Sotheby's (New York)
14. *Forbes* Magazine Galleries (New York)
15. *The Economist* (London)
16. District of Columbia telephone directory, 1985

HEGEMONY (Japanese)

1., 2. Robotics Industries Association (Ann Arbor, Mich.)
3.–5. Mihaly Csikszentmihalyi and Reed Larson, *Being Adolescent: Conflict and Growth in the Teenage Years* (New York: Basic Books, 1986)

6., 7. Seymour Melman, *Profits Without Production* (New York: Alfred A. Knopf, 1983)

8., 9. U.S. Department of Commerce

10., 11. Japanese Ministry of Finance (Tokyo)

12. *American Banker* (New York)

13. Japanese Consulate (New York)

HEGEMONY (Soviet)

1. *Difcom* (Paris)

2., 3. Professor Murray Feshbach, Sovietologist-in-Residence at NATO (Brussels)

4., 5. *Harper's* research

6., 7. *U.S. News and World Report* (Washington, D.C.)

8., 9. *The New York Times*

10. *The Wall Street Journal*

11. Feshbach (see above)

HOSTS AND GUESTS

1.–4. U.S. Immigration and Naturalization Service

5., 6. U.S. Bureau of the Census

7. Prime Minister's Office (Tokyo)

8. U.S. Department of Housing and Urban Development

9. *Weekly Mail* (Johannesburg)

10. *The Progressive* (Madison, Wis.)

11. Captain Brian Thoreson, Walter Reed Medical Center (Washington, D.C.)

ICONOCLASTS

1. Marketing Research Association (Chicago)

2. Direct Marketing Association (New York)

3. Professor Michael Weissman, Department of Physics, University of Illinois (Urbana)

4. Finnish Embassy (Washington, D.C.)

5. *Psychology Today* (Washington, D.C.)

6. Des Moines Register and Tribune Company

7. United Press International (New York)

IDEALS

1. United Press International (New York)
2., 3. Ford Models, Inc. (New York)
4. U.S. Bureau of the Census
5. Roper Organization (New York)
6. *Golf Digest* (Bridgeport, Conn.)

IMPORTS AND EXPORTS

1. *The New Republic* (Washington, D.C.)/International Monetary Fund (Washington, D.C.)
2., 3. International Monetary Fund
4. Japan External Trade Center (New York)
5. First Boston Corporation (New York)
6. U.S. Immigration and Naturalization Service
7. Sea-Land Corporation (Menlo Park, N.J.)
8. Education Council for Foreign Medical Graduates (Philadelphia)
9. National Science Foundation (Washington, D.C.) and National Research Council (Washington, D.C.)

INFRASTRUCTURE

1. Road Information Program (Washington, D.C.)
2. National Institutes of Health (Bethesda, Md.)
3. United Telecom (Kansas City, Mo.)/Charles Berlitz (Fort Lauderdale, Fla.)
4. Commission of Professionals in Science and Technology (Washington, D.C.)
5. "The Grace Commission Report" (U.S. Government Printing Office, 1983)
6., 7. International Monetary Fund (Washington, D.C.)
8., 9. Professor Gary Saxonhouse, Department of Economics, University of Michigan (Ann Arbor)
10. Internal Revenue Service
11. U.S. Department of Energy
12., 13. Earthscan (Washington, D.C.)
14. *Merchandising* (New York)
15. Vanity Fair Mills (Monroeville, Ala.)
16. Roper Organization (New York)

IN KIND

1. Ministry of Trade (Lima, Peru)
2. *The Wall Street Journal*
3. R. L. Polk and Company (Ann Arbor, Mich.)
4. Boot Hill Cemetery and Gift Shop (Tombstone, Ariz.)

INNOCENCE & EXPERIENCE

1. Center for War, Peace and the News Media (New York University) and Roper Organization (New York)
2. Yankelovich Clancy Shulman (Westport, Conn.)
3. Trinity Episcopal School (New York)
4. Stanford University (Stanford, Calif.)
5., 6. Eric Shiviand, Professor of Psychiatry, Massachusetts Institute of Technology (Cambridge)
7., 8. Search Institute (Minneapolis)
9. National Urban League (New York)
10. National Center for Health Statistics (Hyattsville, Md.)
11., 12. Professor Mary Koss, Department of Psychology, Kent State University (Kent, Ohio)
13. Roper Organization (New York)
14., 15. Cocaine Anonymous (Culver City, Calif.)
16. Distilled Spirits Council of the United States (Washington, D.C.)
17. Icelandic Embassy (Washington, D.C.)

IN STEP

1. Tom Gervasi, Center for Military Research and Analysis (Brooklyn)
2. Senate Foreign Relations Committee
3. Larry King Poll (*USA Today*)
4. U.S. Bureau of the Census
5. New York City Ballet
6. Warner-Lambert Company (Morris Plains, N.J.)
7., 8. Levi Strauss & Company (San Francisco) and Gallup Organization (Princeton, N.J.)
9. U.S. Bureau of the Census
10., 11. Bensinger, DuPont and Associates (Chicago)
12. U.S. Highway Traffic Safety Administration

13. Education Commission of the States (Washington, D.C.)
14. Jensen Publications (New Berlin, Wis.)

ISOLATIONISTS

1., 2. Roper Organization (New York)
3. Air Transport Association of America (Washington, D.C.)
4. Motion Picture Association of America (New York)
5. Lender's Bagel Bakery (West Haven, Conn.)
6. *The Atlantic* (Boston)
7., 8. U.S. Bureau of the Census
9. Icelandic Embassy (Washington, D.C.)

JOURNEYS

1. South African Institute of Race Relations (Johannesburg)
2. *The Wall Street Journal*
3., 4. Union of Councils for Soviet Jews (Washington, D.C.)
5., 6. U.S. Coast Guard (Miami)
7. Cuban Mission (New York)
8., 9. U.S. Bureau of the Census
10., 11. Scholl, Inc. (Memphis)
12. R. H. Bruskin (New Brunswick, N.J.)
13. Niagara Falls Public Library
14. *Nester's Official New York Taxi Driver's Guide* (Nester's Map and Guide Company, New York)

JUDGMENTS

1., 2. Roper Organization (New York)
3. Des Moines Register and Tribune Company
4. *Detroit Free Press* and WDIV-TV (Detroit)
5., 6. U.S. Information Agency/Interdisciplinary Consultants on Development (San José, Costa Rica)
7.–10. Gallup Organization (Princeton, N.J.)
11. Daniel Yankelovich, *New Rules: Searching for Self-Fulfillment in a World Turned Upside Down* (New York: Random House, 1982)
12. "Ethan Allen Report: The Status and Future of the American Family" (Danbury, Conn.)

13., 14. Roper Organization (New York)
15., 16. Libel Defense Resource Center (New York)
17., 18. R. H. Bruskin (New Brunswick, N.J.)

LABOR RELATIONS

1., 2. U.S. Bureau of Labor Statistics
3., 4. Louis Harris and Associates (New York)
5. William P. O'Hare, *Poverty in America: Trends and Patterns* (Washington, D.C.: Population Reference Bureau, 1985)
6. Center on Budget and Policy Priorities (Washington, D.C.)
7., 8. U.S. Bureau of Labor Statistics
9. Ivan Carner and Bryna Faser, "Fast Food Jobs" (Washington, D.C.: The Institute for Work and Learning, 1984)
10. Professors Barry Bluestone, Department of Economics, Boston College; and Bennett Harrison, Department of Urban Studies and Planning, Massachusetts Institute of Technology (Cambridge)
11. Washington Analysis Corporation (Washington, D.C.)

LACUNAE

1. National Center for Geographic Education (Macomb, Ill.) and Association of American Geographers (Washington, D.C.)
2. Ernest L. Boyer, *High School* (New York: Harper & Row, 1985)
3. National Association for Educational Progress (Princeton, N.J.)
4. Hearst Corporation (New York) and Research and Forecasts, Inc. (New York)
5. Educational Testing Service (Princeton, N.J.)
6. ABC News (New York) and *Washington Post* Poll
7. *Newsweek* Advertising Resource Center (New York)
8., 9. Media General (Richmond) and Associated Press (New York) Poll

LANDSCAPES

1. French Embassy (Washington, D.C.)
2. New York Department of Parks and Recreation
3. Washington, D.C., Recreation Service
4. *Metropolis* (New York)

110

5. U.S. Government Accounting Office
6. U.S. Department of the Interior
7., 8. National Park Service (Washington, D.C.)
9. U.S. Department of the Interior
10. Bruce Barker, Ivan Muse, and Ralph Smith, "One Teacher Schools in America Today" (Provo, Utah: Brigham Young University College of Education)
11. Society for the Protection of New Hampshire Forests (Concord, N.H.)
12. U.S. Forest Service /U.S. Bureau of the Census/*Harper's* research
13. New York City Tree Consortium
14. Van de Wetering, Inc. (Wading River, N.Y.)
15. James Bissell, Cleveland Museum of Natural History
16. National Research Bureau (Chicago)
17. Gardens for All (Burlington, Vt.) and Gallup Organization (Princeton, N.J.)

LIAISONS

1. *American Psychologist* (Washington, D.C.)
2. Lori Andrews, attorney, American Bar Foundation (Chicago)
3. U.S. Bureau of the Census
4., 5. National Center for Health Statistics (Hyattsville, Md.)
6., 7. Action for Children's Television (Cambridge, Mass.)
8. *Mergers & Acquisitions* (Philadelphia)
9. Professor Robert Reich, Department of Political Economy, Harvard University (Cambridge, Mass.)
10. U.S. State Department
11. Jane Hunter, editor, *Israeli Foreign Affairs Journal* (Oakland)
12., 13. Nicaraguan Central Bank (Managua)
14. Central American Historical Institute (Washington, D.C.)
15. Central Intelligence Agency
16., 17. U.S. Department of Defense

LOST AND FOUND

1., 2. U.S. Department of Defense
3. U.S. Consumer Product Safety Commission

4. Professor Kenzo Sato, Department of Dermatology, University of Iowa College of Medicine (Iowa City)
5. Research Triangle Institute (Research Triangle Park, N.C.)
6. American Journal of Medicine (New York)
7. New York City Police Department
8. Casket Manufacturers Association (Evanston, Ill.)
9. *Business Week* (New York)
10.–12. *U.S. News and World Report* (Washington, D.C.)
13. Beatrix Potter, *The Tale of Timmy Tiptoes* (New York: Frederick Warne & Company, 1911)

MAINSTAYS

1. *Rolling Stone* (New York)
2. New York City Ballet
3. *El País* (Madrid)
4. Irving Berlin Music Company (New York)
5. Broadcast Music, Inc. (New York)
6. *British Business* (London)
7. Town & Country Catering (London)
8. Harry M. Stevens Catering (New York)

MALADIES

1. Health Care Financing Administration (Baltimore)
2. National Center for Health Statistics (Hyattsville, Md.)
3., 4. American Cancer Society (New York)
5. Amateur Athletic Union (Indianapolis)
6. National Center for Health Statistics
7. U.S. Office of Technology Assessment
8., 9. Health Care Financing Administration
10. U.S. Bureau of the Census
11., 12. U.S. Department of Health and Human Services
13. U.S. Senate Committee on Labor and Human Resources

MANNERS

1. American Telephone and Telegraph Company (New York)
2., 3. *Family Circle* (New York)
4., 5. U.S. Bureau of the Census
6., 7. Simmons Market Research Bureau (New York)

112

8. *Marie-Claire* (Paris)
9., 10. Ann Landers (Chicago)
11. Search Institute (Minneapolis)
12. Louis Harris and Associates (New York)
13. *The Times* (London)
14. British Agricultural Ministry (London)
15., 16. *The New England Journal of Medicine* (Boston)

MARKETS

1. Holstein Association (Brattleboro, Vt.)
2. Idant Corporation (New York)
3. Surrogate Parenting, Inc. (Louisville, Ky.)
4. Michael H. Minton with Jean L. Bloch, *What is a Wife Worth?* (New York: William Morrow, 1983)
5. *The Washington Post Weekly*
6. *SIPRI Yearbook, 1986* (New York: Oxford University Press)
7. Robert Harris, *Selling Hitler* (New York: Pantheon Books, 1986)
8.–10. *The Wall Street Journal*
11. *Harper's* research
12. *The Face* (London)
13. *Newsweek* (New York)
14. Chicago Title Insurance Company
15., 16. *Psychology Today* (Washington, D.C.)
17. Citizens' Research Foundation (Los Angeles)/Committee for the Study of the American Electorate (Washington, D.C.)
18. U.S. Occupational Safety and Health Administration
19. U.S. Federal Aviation Administration

MEDIA

1. Hay Group (Philadelphia)
2. Lawrence Weschler, *The New Yorker*
3. Soviet Embassy (Washington, D.C.)
4. Newspaper Advertising Bureau (New York)/Magazine Publishers Association (New York)/U.S. Bureau of the Census
5. Greeting Card Association (Washington, D.C.)
6. National Assessment of Education Progress (Princeton, N.J.)
7.–9. *The New York Times*
10., 11. Ford Motor Company (Dearborn, Mich.)

MOVEMENTS

1., 2. U.S. Bureau of the Census
3. Voter Education Project (Atlanta)
4. Department of Trade and Industry (London)
5., 6. Professor Michael Hill, Department of Sociology, University of Minnesota (Duluth)
7., 8. Athletics Congress (Indianapolis)
9., 10. *American Demographics* (Ithaca, N.Y.)

MUTANTS

1., 2. Professor George P. Georgehiou, Department of Entomology, University of California (Riverside)
3. U.S. Patent Office
4. Daniel's Clover Specialty Company (St. Petersburg, Fla.)
5. Robotic Industries Association (Ann Arbor, Mich.)
6. National Institute for Occupational Safety and Health (Atlanta)

MYSTERIES

1. U.S. Department of Justice
2., 3. R. H. Bruskin (New Brunswick, N.J.)
4. U.S. Marshal Service (Department of Justice)
5. U.S. Government Accounting Office, *Information and Personnel Security: Data on Employees Affected by Federal Security Programs* (U.S. Government Printing Office, 1986)
6., 7. Audits and Surveys (San Francisco)

NOSTRUMS

1. Public Agenda Foundation (New York)
2. National Opinion Research Center (Chicago)

OBSERVANCES

1. Graceland (Memphis)
2., 3. Otto Harrassowitz, book dealer (Wiesbaden, West Germany)
4. New American Library (New York)
5. *The Times* (London)

114

6. United Nations (New York)
7. Des Moines Register and Tribune Company
8. Senate Democratic Policy Committee/National Archives (Washington, D.C.)
9., 10. Professor Sheldon Goldman, Department of Political Science, University of Massachusetts (Amherst)
11., 12. Gallup Organization (Princeton, N.J.)
13. National Restaurant Association (Washington, D.C.)
14. U.S. Occupational Safety and Health Administration

ODDS

1., 2. National Climatic Data Center (Asheville, N.C.)
3. Benevolent and Protective Order of Elks (Bismarck, N.D.)
4. Werner Erhard and Associates (San Francisco)
5. U.S. House Subcommittee on Health and Long-term Care
6. American Bar Association (Chicago)
7., 8. Professors Neil G. Bennett and Patricia Craig, Department of Sociology, Yale University (New Haven, Conn.); and David E. Bloom, Department of Economics, Harvard University (Cambridge, Mass.)
9. U.S. Bureau of the Census

OMENS

1. *The New Republic* (Washington, D.C.)
2. *South* (London)
3. West Bank Data Base Project (Jerusalem)
4. Polish Police Academy (Warsaw)
5., 6. U.S. Bureau of Labor Statistics
7. First Boston Corporation (New York)

ORNAMENTS

1. Career Blazers (New York)
2. Harvard University (Cambridge, Mass.)
3. Bert Sugar (Chappaqua, N.Y.), former editor, *Ring*
4. *Defense and Foreign Affairs* (Washington, D.C.)
5., 6. *Limousine and Chauffeur* (Redondo Beach, Calif.)
7. Florida Alligator Farmers Association (Orlando)/Louisiana Department of Wildlife and Fisheries (Baton Rouge)

8. Filipino Presidential Commission on Good Government (New York)
9. *Harper's* research
10. Coalition of Labor Union Women (New York)

PASTIMES

1. *Forbes* (New York)
2. *Journal Français d'Amérique* (San Francisco)
3. *The New York Times*
4. Toy Manufacturers of America (New York)
5. American Bowling Congress (Greendale, Wis.)
6., 7. Tom Biracree, *How You Rate: Women* (New York: Dell Publishing, 1984)
8. A. C. Nielsen (New York)
9. MRCA Information Services (Northbrook, Ill.)
10., 11. American Cancer Society (New York)

PLOYS

1. B-1 System Program Office, Wright-Patterson Air Force Base (Dayton)
2. William M. Arkin and Richard W. Fieldhouse, *Nuclear Battlefields: Global Links in the Arms Race* (Boston: Ballinger, 1985)
3. Federation of American Scientists (Washington, D.C.)
4., 5. The Unemployment Unit (London)
6. Public Citizen's Congress Watch (Washington, D.C.)
7. *The Wall Street Journal*
8. U.S. Treasury Department
9. Trans Time (Oakland)

PRIORITIES

1., 2. University of Alabama (Tuscaloosa)
3., 4. Drug Abuse Policy Office (White House)
5.–7. "Annual Report of the Department of National Education" (Pretoria)
8., 9. "The American Freshman" (American Council of Education, and University of California at Los Angeles)
10. "Notre Dame Study of Catholic Parish Life" (Notre Dame, Ind.)

116

11., 12. Gallup Organization (Princeton, N.J.) and Council for Applied Research in the Apostolate (Washington, D.C.)

13., 14. Tom Biracree, *How You Rate: Women* (New York: Dell Publishing, 1984)

15. Oxtoby-Smith (New York)

16., 17. McGraw-Hill Economics (New York)

18. U.S. Department of Defense/*The Advocate National Gay News Magazine* (Los Angeles)/*Harper's* research

19. U.S. Congressional Arts Caucus

20. U.S. Office of Management and Budget

PROCEDURES

1. *Population Bulletin* (Population Reference Bureau, Washington, D.C.)

2. Alan Guttmacher Institute (New York)

3. New York City Department of Health

4. Medic II program (Seattle Fire Department)

5. Amnesty International (New York)

6. Professor Giorgio Solimano, School of Public Health, Columbia University (New York)

7., 8. *Science* (Washington, D.C.)/Institute of Medicine (Washington, D.C.)

9., 10. Edward A. Wallerstein, medical writer (New York)

11. *Elle* (Paris)

12. *Asahi Shimbun* (Tokyo)

13. U.S. Department of Agriculture

QUOTIDIA

1. Tom Parker, *In One Day* (Boston: Houghton Mifflin, 1984)

2. John Love, *McDonald's: Behind the Arches* (New York: Bantam, 1986)

3. Roper Organization (New York)

4. MRCA Information Services (Northbrook, Ill.)

5.–8. Roper Organization (New York)

9. Muzak Group W Westinghouse (New York)

10., 11. U.S. Bureau of Labor Statistics

12. Roper Organization (New York)

13. *American Journal of Public Health* (Washington, D.C.)

REALPOLITIK

1. Michael Kidron and Dan Smith, *The State of War Atlas: Armed Conflict—Armed Peace* (New York: Simon & Schuster, 1983)
2. U.S. Arms Control and Disarmament Agency
3. Associated Press (New York)
4., 5. U.S. Department of Commerce
6. U.S. Department of Energy
7. Rock Creek Research (Washington, D.C.)
8., 9. *Directory of U.S. Firms Operating in Foreign Countries,* 10th Edition (New York: World Trade Academy Press, 1984)
10. South African Institute of Race Relations (Johannesburg)
11., 12. Democratic National Convention (Washington, D.C.)
13. *Chicago Reporter*
14. Lynn Margulis and Dorion Sagan, *Microcosmos* (New York: Summit Books, 1986)

RECEIVABLES

1. Internal Revenue Service
2. Paul S. Richter, attorney for G. Gordon Liddy (Washington, D.C.)
3. Committee on Governmental Affairs: "Collection of Criminal Fines" (U.S. Government Printing Office, 1984)
4. U.S. Bureau of the Census

REVOLUTION (Post-Industrial)

1. Cleveland Clinic Foundation
2. The American Fertility Society (Birmingham, Ala.)
3. *The New England Journal of Medicine* (Boston)
4. *Harper's* research
5. International Business Machines (Armonk, N.Y.)
6. *Perspectives in Biology and Medicine* (Chicago: University of Chicago Press, Autumn 1980)
7., 8. Management Practice Consulting Partners (New York)
9. Carroon and Black in Space (Washington, D.C.)
10. LINK (New York)
11. Louis Harris and Associates (New York)

REVOLUTION (Reagan)

1. U.S. Bureau of Labor Statistics
2. Professor Sheldon Goldman, Department of Political Science, University of Massachusetts (Amherst)
3. U.S. Office of Management and Budget
4., 5. "Economic Report of the President, 1985" (U.S. Government Printing Office)
6., 7. Data Resources (Lexington, Mass.)
8., 9. U.S. Department of Defense
10. *National Journal* (Washington, D.C.)
11. Council on Economic Priorities (New York)
12., 13. Physicians for Social Responsibility (Washington, D.C.)

REVOLUTION (Sexual)

1., 2. Needham, Harper & Steers (Chicago)
3., 4. The Conference Board (New York)
5. Phyllis Chesler, *Mothers on Trial: The Battle for Children and Custody* (New York: McGraw-Hill, 1986)
6. Academy of Matrimonial Lawyers (Chicago)
7., 8. *USA Today*
9. New York Stock Exchange
10., 11. Needham, Harper & Steers (Chicago)
12. U.S. Bureau of Labor Statistics
13. AFL-CIO (Washington, D.C.)
14. U.S. Department of Justice
15., 16. *The Wall Street Journal* and Gallup Organization (Princeton, N.J.)
17., 18. National Institutes of Health

RISKS

1. Zimbabwean Mission (New York)
2. Congressional Research Service
3. U.S. Department of Justice
4. U.S. Securities and Exchange Commission
5., 6. *Venture* (New York)
7., 8. Salomon Brothers (New York)
9. Internal Revenue Service

10. U.S. Bureau of Justice Statistics
11. U.S. Bureau of Justice Statistics
12. Julie K. Ehrhart and Bernice R. Sandler, "Campus Gang Rape: Party Games?" (Washington, D.C.: Association of American Colleges, 1985)
13., 14. National Clearinghouse on Marital Rape (Berkeley, Calif.)
15., 16. Mine Safety and Health Administration (Arlington, Va.)/National Safety Council (Chicago)
17. National Science Foundation (Washington, D.C.)
18. California Department of Insurance (Sacramento)
19. Nuclear Regulatory Commission (Washington, D.C.)
20. Iowa Geological Survey (Iowa City)
21. National Institute of Environmental Health Sciences (Research Triangle Park, N.C.)
22. Vance Research Services (Lincolnshire, Ill.)

RITES (of Passage)

1. Timex Corporation (Waterbury, Conn.)
2., 3. Dr. J. M. Tanner, *Growth at Adolescence* (Springfield, Ill.: Charles Thomas, 1962)
4., 5. U.S. Department of Justice
6., 7. Planned Parenthood Federation of America (New York)
8., 9. Robert Coles and Geoffrey Stokes, *Sex and the American Teenager* (New York: Harper & Row, 1985)
10. John F. Love, *McDonald's: Behind the Arches* (New York: Bantam Books, 1986)
11. National Center for Health Statistics (Hyattsville, Md.)
12. Little Church of the West (Las Vegas)

SECOND THOUGHTS

1., 2. National Center for Education Statistics (Washington, D.C.)/National Education Association (Washington, D.C.)
3., 4. Department of Employment (London)
5. R. H. Bruskin (New Brunswick, N.J.)
6. Barbara Keating and Kelley M. L. Brigman, "Gay and Bisexual Fathers" (Mankato, Minn.: Mankato State University Department of Sociology, 1985)
7. U.S. Senate Select Committee on Intelligence

SENTIMENTS

1. Greeting Card Association (Washington, D.C.)
2. Roses, Inc. (Haslett, Mich.)
3. Greeting Card Association (Washington, D.C.)
4., 5. *Chicago Sun-Times*
6. S&G (Milan)
7. Media General (Richmond) and Associated Press (New York) Poll
8. Gallup Youth Survey (Princeton, N.J.)
9., 10. "Eurobarometer" (Brussels: Commission of the European Communities, 1986)
11. Des Moines Register and Tribune Company
12. Roper Organization (New York)
13. R. H. Bruskin (New Brunswick, N.J.)

STANDARDS AND PRACTICES

1. NBC News (New York) and *The Wall Street Journal* Poll
2. Federal Highway Administration (Washington, D.C.)
3. New York Police Department
4. Los Angeles Police Department
5. Elizabeth Pond, *From the Yaroslavsky Station* (New York: Universe Books, 1984)
6., 7. *The Washington Post*
8. *Journal of Communications* (Philadelphia)
9. U.S. General Accounting Office
10. U.S. Senate Select Committee on Ethics
11. U.S. Food and Drug Administration
12., 13. Family Research Laboratory (University of New Hampshire, Durham)

SUBTRACTIONS

1. Footwear Industries of America (Arlington, Va.)
2., 3. Casket Manufacturers Association of America (Evanston, Ill.)
4. British House of Lords
5. Embassy of the People's Republic of China (Washington, D.C.)
6., 7. Americas Watch (New York)
8., 9. American Medical Association (Chicago)
10., 11. National Center for Health Statistics (Hyattsville, Md.)

12. Professor Dave Pimentel, Department of Entymology and Agricultural Sciences, Cornell University (Ithaca, N.Y.)
13. George P. Mochis, "A Study of Juvenile Shoplifting," Department of Marketing (unpublished paper, Georgia State University, Atlanta)

SUPERSTITIONS

1., 2. National Opinion Research Center (Chicago)
3. Committee for the Scientific Investigation of Claims of the Paranormal (Buffalo)
4. American Astronomical Society (Washington, D.C.)
5. American Federation of Astrologers (Tempe, Ariz.)
6. *Scientific American* (Boston)
7., 8. American Council on Science and Health (New York)
9. National Insurance Consumer Organization (Alexandria, Va.)
10. Miller Brewing Company Survey (Milwaukee)
11. Erlendur Haraldsson, *National Survey of Psychic Phenomena and Religious and Paranormal Beliefs* (Reykjavik: University of Iceland Department of Psychology, 1974)

SUSPICIONS

1., 2. Louis Harris and Associates (New York)
3. Administrative Office of the U.S. Courts (Washington, D.C.)
4. U.S. Government Accounting Office
5. National Organization for the Reform of Marijuana Laws (Washington, D.C.)
6., 7. *Security Letter* (New York)
8. Information Security Oversight Office (U.S. General Services Administration)
9. U.S. State Department
10. ABC News (New York) and *Washington Post* Poll
11. *Manchester Guardian Weekly*
12. Committee for the Scientific Investigation of Claims of the Paranormal (Buffalo)
13. Gallup Organization (Princeton, N.J.)

TALK

1. White House
2. U.S. Consumer Product Safety Commission

3., 4. Robin Weir (Washington, D.C.)
5. Lee Iacocca (Detroit)
6. Mario Cuomo (Albany, N.Y.)
7. Peter L. Benson and Dorothy L. Williams, *Religion on Capitol Hill: Myths and Realities* (New York: Harper & Row, 1982)
8. *The New York Times*
9. U.S. Department of Defense
10. Voice of America (Washington, D.C.)/Radio Free Europe (Washington, D.C.)
11. Radio Free Europe
12. *Times Mirror* (Los Angeles) and Gallup Organization (Princeton, N.J.) Poll
13. U.S. Bureau of the Census
14. Adam Robinson (New York)/*Princeton Review* (New York)
15. Roper Organization (New York)

TASKS

1. Recognition Equipment, Inc. (Dallas)
2. Accountemps (New York)
3. Western U.S. Lifesaving Association (Huntington Beach, Calif.)
4. Association of the U.S. Army, "Peace in Peril" (Arlington, Va.: Association of the United States Army, 1983)
5. *Washington Post*
6. U.S. Naval Institute (Annapolis, Md.)
7. Rod McKuen (Beverly Hills, Calif.)
8. Pepsico (Purchase, N.Y.)/*Harper's* research
9. Professor Antonio DaMasio, Department of Neurology, University of Iowa College of Medicine (Iowa City)
10. Tax Foundation, Inc. (Washington, D.C.)
11. Richard L. Rosenthal, *Reform? or A Rational Tax System* (Stamford, Conn.: Citizen's Utilities, 1981)
12. *Science News* (Washington, D.C.)

TRANSIENTS

1., 2. *Information Please Almanac Atlas and Yearbook, 1986* (Boston: Houghton Mifflin)
3. Swiss Embassy (Washington, D.C.)
4., 5. National Association of Temporary Services (Alexandria, Va.)

123

6. Runzheimer International (Rochester, Wis.)
7. Professor David F. Sly, director, and Muhammed Bailey, Center for the Study of Population, Florida State University (Tallahassee)
8. *Permanent Homelessness in America* (Cambridge, Mass.: National Bureau of Economic Research, 1986)
9. J. D. Power & Associates (Westlake Village, Calif.)
10. U.S. Bureau of the Census
11. Association of American Railroads (Washington, D.C.)

WAYS AND MEANS

1. Rand Corporation (Santa Monica, Calif.)
2., 3. NAACP Legal Defense and Educational Fund (New York)
4. President's Commission for the Study of Ethical Problems in Medicine: "Deciding to Forgo Life-Sustaining Treatment: A Report on the Study of Ethical, Medical, and Legal Issues in Treatment Decisions" (U.S. Government Printing Office, 1983)
5–7. *Harper's* research
8. *American Journal of Public Health* (Washington, D.C.)

WINDFALLS

1., 2. Tom Gervasi, Center for Military Research and Analysis (Brooklyn, N.Y.)
3. *Los Angeles Herald Examiner*
4. Laventhol and Horwath, *U.S. Gaming Industry* (Los Angeles: Laventhol & Horwath, 1986)/*Harper's* research
5. George Bush's 1985 Financial Disclosure Report

WORRIES

1. "Situational Determinants of Shyness," by Professors Warren Jones, Department of Psychology, University of Tulsa; and Dan Russell, Department of Psychology, University of Iowa College of Medicine (Iowa City)
2., 3. *Teenage* (New York)
4., 5. DDB Needham Worldwide (New York)
6. Professor Thomas Borkovec, Department of Psychology, Pennsylvania State University (State College, Pa.)

7., 8. Tom Biracree, *How You Rate: Women* (New York: Dell Publishing, 1984)
9. Runzheimer International (Rochester, Wis.)
10. Kepner-Tregoe (Princeton, N.J.)

YIELDS

1., 2. Data Resources, Inc. (New York)
3. U.S. Department of Agriculture/National Organization for the Reform of Marijuana Laws (Washington, D.C.)
4. National Gardening Association (Burlington, Vt.)
5. United Nations World Food Council (New York)
6., 7. National Marine Fisheries Service (St. Petersburg, Fla.)
8., 9. Oceanside Holiday Inn (Fort Lauderdale, Fla.)
10., 11. Tom Parker, *In One Day* (Boston: Houghton Mifflin, 1984)
12. Commercial Service Systems (Van Nuys, Calif.)
13. *American Demographics* (Ithaca, N.Y.)
14. National Football League (New York)
15., 16. National and American Leagues of Professional Baseball (New York)

ZEROS

1. *Fortune* (New York)
2. *Harper's* research
3. G. P. Putnam & Sons (New York)
4. Dell Publishing Co. (New York)
5. Runzheimer International (Rochester, Wis.)